The Archers
ANNUAL 2000
KATE WILLMOTT and HEDLI NIKLAUS

AMBRIDGE FUN AND GAMES WITH
A REVIEW OF EVENTS IN 1999 AND A
TANTALISING GLIMPSE OF WHAT
IS TO COME!

Hello

I was delighted with the idea of an *Archers Annual* so I'm especially pleased to be asked to write the foreword for the very first one. I found it a great read, packed with interesting facts, a look behind the scenes, activities and fun for all the family. (I'm still working on Stephen Fry's crossword!) It'll make a great present for an 'Addict' you know, a treat for a friend or perhaps you are simply treating yourself to a copy. Whatever your reason for buying this book, I am sure it will provide hours of reading pleasure.

Making *The Archers* is a fast and complex business. On any one day there could be up to seven Archers cycles in progress. An episode of *The Archers* is on air; an episode is being edited for later transmission; an episode is being recorded in studio, with actors, director and technicians; an episode, recently written, is being script edited by myself or a senior producer; four episodes are being written by four of our team of writers; sound effects are being gathered for *The Archers* scripts next in studio, and finally storylines are being researched in time for the next *Archers* script meeting.

Then, of course, we have all the publicity and promotional activities that go alongside running a daily serial. There's the casting of new characters, the long-term planning meetings, the answering of listeners' letters, and from time to time we meet the fans at Archers Conventions and Roadshows.

Inside these pages you will get an insight into the busy world of Ambridge. I do hope you enjoy it.

Vanessa Whitburn
Editor, *The Archers*

THEY CAUGHT IT OFF LYNDA SNELL

FOOT IN MOUTH DISEASE

Contents

Welcome to

Birmingham

Reception

WHERE IS A

YOUR EXCLUSIVE STUDIO VISIT STARTS HERE

Reception

Collect your visitor's pass.

BBC
VISITOR'S PASS

Name
Date
Studio
         BBC Birmingham

Green Room

The actors gather in a small room with low tables and easy chairs to read through their scripts together before they go into Studio 3 to record an episode. Pictures of the cast, past and present, line the walls of the Green Room (the theatrical name for a backstage lounge), and there are usually stacks of photographs and cards for cast members to sign for *Archers* fans.

STUDIO

Every house, street or field of Ambridge can be evoked in Studio 3, thanks to a few carefully designed permanent fixtures.

Ups and Downs

A seemingly pointless staircase in a corner of the studio leads to a door which opens but goes nowhere, covered with every conceivable type of latch and doorknob (see opposite page). A third of the steps are stone, a third are metal 'fire escape' stairs, and the rest are wooden or carpeted,

so that footsteps can sound soft or hard, depending on where the character is supposed to be.

MBRIDGE?

IN THE HEART OF BIRMINGHAM!

specific Ambridge locations. Scenes at the Bull and the kitchens of Bridge Farm and Home Farm are recorded near the sink; the living rooms and Grey Gables reception are recorded in the centre of the studio, and there's a hard floor for the village hall or Pat's dairy.

There's also a refrigerator, a stove, several tables and some chairs that are pressed into regular use, along with a bed which is wheeled out for the steamier love scenes.

BRIGHT LIGHTS

Green cue lights inside and a blue light outside the studio show that everyone is rehearsing, but a red light means that recording is taking place. No-one enters the studio as it could ruin a scene which would then have to be re-recorded.

Water, water everywhere

It may look like something from a museum of bad plumbing, but thanks to the magic of radio this cracked old sink can be transformed into a river, a fountain, a swimming pool or a kitchen. Every time you hear running water in *The Archers*, it's coming out of one of these taps. The sink is usually piled high with crockery to create the sound of washing-up.

Where am I?

Different areas of the studio are used to create the right ambience for the

Behind the scenes

The soundproofed control room is located behind several thicknesses of heavy glass along one side of the studio. The production team can see the actors, and vice versa, but sound travels between them by microphone only, so that the technical crew hear exactly what will be recorded for the listening audience. The state-of-the-art mixing desk (below) allows the director to co-ordinate all the disparate sound elements into one smoothly running episode.

THE GREAT OUTDOORS

Open spaces in Ambridge are recorded in what's called a 'dead' room, an enclosed area with soft surfaces which kill any echo. Sound doesn't reverberate outside, so if you're pulling leeks (below right), hanging out the washing or shouting across a field, you'll be put in *The Archers'* very own padded cell.

What's that noise?

The actors have their hands busy holding their scripts, so any extra sounds have to be provided by the 'spot effects' person. So if there are teacups to be rattled, washing-up to be done, vegetables to be chopped or presents to be opened, 'spot' races into action with the necessary tools of the trade. A champagne bottle to be opened? No problem: simply take a bicycle pump, a piece of string and a cork. Voilà! Instant celebration!

Below: *Pulling leeks at Brookfield*

IMPORTANT PEOPLE

The **senior studio manager** is responsible for the technical side of the recording: balancing voices and effects, listening to the director and following the script as he or she sits at the mixing desk in the control room. Another studio manager feeds in pre-recorded sound effects, some recorded specifically for a particular episode. Birdsong, a crying baby, the arrival of a van, all have to be carefully integrated and entirely appropriate for the occasion if complaints from sharp-eared listeners are to be avoided.

The **director** and assistant sit near the control desk and are in constant contact with the studio manager. Closed-circuit television enables them to see what's happening in distant corners of the studio and to check that everyone's in the right place at the right time. They can communicate with the actors by using a 'talk-back' microphone.

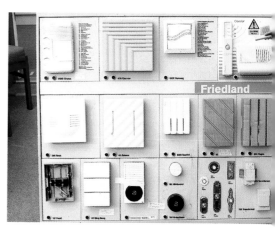

Ding dong! All the bells of Ambridge on one handy board

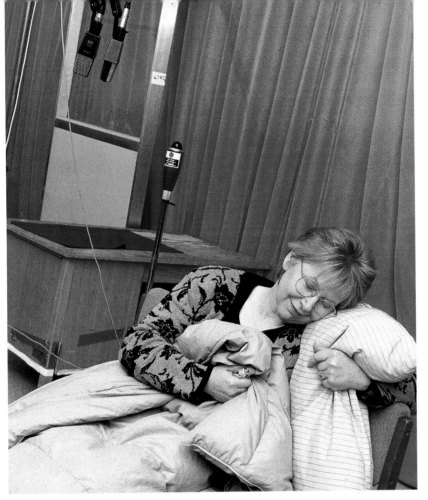

Hedli Niklaus, who plays Bull landlady Kathy Perks, records a bed scene (left); actors rehearse a scene between takes (above); a busy corner of Studio 3 (below)

SOUNDS DELIGHTFUL

All you need to recreate the birth of a lamb on radio is a pot of yoghurt, some old recording tape and a damp towel.

A LOVER'S GUIDE

In the chaste 50s, kissing noises were created by actors kissing the back of their own hand. Now, however, recording techniques are so sensitive that only the real thing will do.

Clockwise from above: *The master clock shows exactly when recording is in process; sound effects tapes are lined up ready for use; Hedli runs riot in the spot effects store; the Brookfield Aga nestles underneath the studio stairs; the spot effects technician gets to work with some leeks while Tom Graham (Tommy Archer) concentrates on his lines.*

HOW DID THEY DO THAT?

1950

The Archers has always been pre-recorded, like practically every other radio drama. Pilot editions on the Midland Home Service were cut directly on to large 16-inch discs that were played back at 33⅓ rpm, using a stylus similar to an old-fashioned gramophone needle. Mistakes had to be kept to a minimum as any retakes meant using another disc – an expensive and time-consuming business.

1952

Discs were quickly replaced by magnetic tape, and heavy EMI machines were used both for recording and playback on the Light Programme. The tape, on large spools, gave a much better sound quality than the old discs, and could be edited by a simpler process of cutting and splicing. So-called 'midget' recorders (which weighed a lot) were dragged outside to record location sound effects.

1971

Production of *The Archers* moved from the original BBC Birmingham studios at 282 Broad Street to a new drama suite at BBC Pebble Mill a year before the building was officially opened. Studio 3 had purpose-built, up-to-date facilities. At last the cast had a green room and didn't have to climb two flights of stairs to reach the studio.

1992

By now, most radio drama was being recorded in stereo and *The Archers*, on Radio 4, followed suit. The cast had to learn new microphone techniques to cope with the enhanced realism of stereo, and a new stereo version of *Barwick Green*, the famous *Archers* theme tune, had to be recorded.

1996

A brand new computerised editing system, affectionately known as SADIE (Studio Audio Digital Editor), makes it much easier for the producer to take out 'fluffs' and drop in sound effects. All the editing is now done on screen, rather than by the old method of cutting and sticking tape. At the end of the century *The Archers* is a completely digital production. DAT tape offers the best possible sound, and several episodes can be fitted on a single cassette that is no larger than a matchbox.

Stars in their Ears

Every Archers fan has a favourite character, one they secretly admire or feel most in tune with. Here, some of our most distinguished listeners reveal who they'd most like to be – and why

Alice Beer

Debbie Aldridge. Things have been very quiet for Debbie, and she seems to do nothing but worry. I think there could be a big love interest in the offing. Perhaps Dr Hathaway?

Alan Titchmarsh

Jack Woolley – because he is totally impossible but can't see it, *and* he gets to organise an estate and drive about in a Bentley. Oh, yes! I could do that.

Wendy Richard

This is a difficult one. Be Lynda Snell and risk getting slapped by someone? Be Clarrie and risk not being able to slap Eddie or Joe? I think I'll settle for **Elizabeth.** Nigel is a sweetie, and Mrs Pargetter is definitely up for a slap from her daughter-in-law. The way things are going, Helen is high on the slapometer too! Hayley's fab!

Ned Sherrin

I'd like to be any character who is entitled to put Helen Archer over their knee and spank her. Poor Hayley.

Norma Major

Jill Archer – we seem to share so many of the same values.

Adam Faith

I'd like to be **Nelson's long-lost brother**. This would enable me to realise a major ambition in my life – to play a part in the series.

Joanna Trollope

I'd be **Clarrie Grundy**. She has an exhausting life, but she is the linchpin for all those useless men around her, and liked and admired for it. She has terrific spirit as well as a warm heart. I really, somehow, *believe* in her.

ON THE PSYCH

CLARRIE GRUNDY EXPLORES HER PSYCHE WITH CELEBRITY SHRINK DR CHARLES YOUNG

CHARLES Clarrie, you were picked for this celebratory millennium interview as a result of a competition.

CLARRIE Yes, that's right. I thought I were goin' to win a new suite … ooh, we could really do with a new one of them. I don't suppose you give away any prizes, do you?

CHARLES Now, Clarrie – you were born in 1954. Your father worked most of his life as a farm labourer, your mother looked after the house. Would you say that yours was a traditional upbringing?

CLARRIE Well, we always had a turkey on the table at Christmas. Mind you, I wouldn't care if I never saw a turkey again. I must have plucked thousands and thousands of the beggars.

CHARLES But your father was the head of the household?

CLARRIE You're dead right there. You didn't get on the wrong side of my Dad if you could help it.

CHARLES You were a bright girl and left school with a number of good passes in your 'O' levels at the age of sixteen. Would you like to have stayed on to do your 'A' levels?

CLARRIE Oh you do talk beautifully, just like Mr Pemberton used to – poor soul – he's dead now! Course if you marry someone half your age what can you expect? And his son was no better than he should have been. Drove his poor Dad into an early grave if you ask me. And Caroline all on her own in that huge Dower House, when's she going to meet someone else, that's what I'd like to know.

CHARLES For the moment Clarrie let's return to your story. You're quite a fighter, aren't you?

CLARRIE Well, I give the boys a clout from time to time. But only when they deserves it.

CHARLES I'm talking about when you tackled your father's boss, Phil Archer, and told him that he should sort out your mother's kitchen at Woodbine Cottage which your parents rented from Mr Archer. That was a very brave thing to do.

CLARRIE Oh that. Well if I'd known what was to come of it I'd never 'ave done it, would I? You could say that was my life's biggest mistake.

CHARLES And how's that?

CLARRIE That's when I met my Eddie.

CHARLES Your husband Eddie Grundy?

CLARRIE That's the one. I should have realised then what I was in for – when he told me the range was new. I were that annoyed when I found out it was secondhand. He hasn't changed.

CHARLES What was it about him that you found most attractive?

CLARRIE Well, it wasn't his horns if that's what you're thinking. No, it were his songs. In them days my Eddie were really romantic. He sang me lovely songs. They used to make me cry and cry! I'd 'ave done anything for him, I would.

CHARLES So he wooed you with song and after a whirlwind courtship you got married just a year later.

CLARRIE I weren't expecting or anything, so don't you go thinking that. And it weren't as easy as you make it sound. In the end I had to pay him to get him up the altar.

CHARLES Pay him?

CLARRIE He got into terrible debt trying to launch his career as a Country & Western star so I seized me chance and said I'd pay it off if he married me. Bit like one of them stories Mrs Pargetter's so keen on – like The Bartered Bride only this time it were more a case of The Bartered Bridegroom. That reminds me of Tom Cruise, when he came to make a film at Lower Loxley Hall. He kissed me, you know. Ooh, wouldn't I just fancy being one of them heroines with palpitating bosoms if he were the Lord of the manor.

He'd be all stern and masterful, with those flashing blue eyes, and I'd just melt into his arms and he would give me a slow passionate kiss. And then, just as he was about to ravish me...

CHARLES Yes?

CLARRIE Eddie would turn up wanting his tea.

CHARLES We must mention the big adventure of your life, when you and Eddie decided to leave your roots in Ambridge and start a new life in France.

CLARRIE Oh it were wonderful over there. We had to come back in the end but I loved it. Truth is you'd have to go with someone like Jean Paul, not Eddie. Someone who drinks wine and likes the food, and isn't always asking for a beer every two seconds. Then you could look at the sights in peace and go for long walks by the Seine. Eddie kept wanting to dredge it for treasure.

CHARLES Clarrie, the picture you paint of Eddie makes me wonder whether you have ever thought of leaving him.

CLARRIE Me? Leave my Eddie? I couldn't do that!

CHARLES Why not?

CLARRIE What would he do without me to wash and cook for him, and mind Joe,

and cheer him up when he's down? There ain't an inch of malice in him. He does ever such a lot of good turns for people, and I don't care what people say, he's a good father to our two boys and a good son to Joe. I thought you were ever so nice to start off with, Charles, with your lovely voice and accent and everything but if you think I've come here to listen to you badmouth my Eddie you've got another think coming!

CHARLES I certainly never intended to suggest that Eddie –

CLARRIE And another thing. He wrote a song for me, special that is, it's called Clarrie's Song. Has anyone written a song for you?

CHARLES Well, no.

CLARRIE There you are then.

CHARLES Clarrie, thank you for opening yourself up to me. It's been a tremendous pleasure.

CLARRIE Ta.

What Debbie Did Next...

Affairs with older men, fatal accidents, domestic violence – all in a day's work for Ambridge's Everywoman, Debbie Aldridge. As she takes centre stage in a major storyline, we take an in-depth look at a murky past and (over the page) a brighter future

TEN THINGS EVERY DEBBIE ALDRIDGE FAN OUGHT TO KNOW

1. The daughter of Roger and Jennifer Travers-Macy, she was known as Debbie Macy when her parents divorced. She later took the name of Aldridge which pleased her stepfather Brian.

2. She went to Exeter University to read French and English but returned to Home Farm half-way through her course. She'd been on the verge of running away to Canada with her tutor, Simon Gerrard, when he left her for another woman.

3. She turned down an offer to become Nelson Gabriel's partner in his antique business, preferring to work on the farm.

4. She got the sharp end of Brian's tongue when he expected her to deliver results from the Courses for Horses scheme she had set up. She soon learned to manage the fishing lake and the off-the-road riding course.

5. A surprise guest asked for her at her 21st Birthday Lunch at Grey Gables. Jennifer followed Debbie to the rendezvous at Nelson's Wine Bar, and discovered she was meeting her natural father Roger. A shiny new car followed as a present from him.

6. Debbie and sister Kate were held hostage in the village shop by Clive Horrobin and his gang. Memories of the event took a long time to fade.

7. In 1994 Mark Hebden drove into a tree to avoid Debbie and Caroline Bone on horseback. He was killed, and Debbie was consumed with guilt.

8. She has searched for her perfect partner in all walks of life, from tutor Simon to Dr Locke, from landowner Simon Pemberton to farm worker Steve Oakley.

9. She was awarded the paltry sum of £150 when she took her one-time boyfriend Simon Pemberton to court for beating her up. He pleaded guilty to a charge of Assault Occasioning Actual Bodily Harm, and fled the country.

10. Debbie has taken a big step by moving in with her lover Simon Gerrard. How will this affect her already strained relationship with Brian? Will Debbie continue to work on the farm? And might Simon eventually tempt her away to Canada, as nearly happened once before?

Debbie 💔 Simon

SMOULDERING LOVE AFFAIRS

Considering the number of love affairs that go on in Ambridge, not to mention the much talked-about pregnancies, it's hard to find someone who's left out. Even the glimpse of an old black-and-white photo of Walter Gabriel with Mrs P acts as a reminder of a once smouldering passion. Yet Debbie Aldridge's cool poise drives her lovers distracted as they try to get closer, for Debbie has long mastered the art of the perfect put-down.

WALKING ALONE

28-year-old Debbie Aldridge of Home Farm is not without friends male or female, works for her stepfather on the farm, is a close friend and confidante of Elizabeth Pargetter, is eager to help someone in need, as Neil Carter or William Grundy would testify; yet, like a cat she gives the appearance of always walking alone. There was a hint of attraction between Debbie and her stepfather's gamekeeper Greg Turner, but it never went beyond a friendly drink.

AFFAIR OF THE HEART

It takes a mother to know her daughter, and Jennifer was well aware that an affair of the heart was behind Debbie's decision to give up her degree course at Exeter University and return to the family farm. All that Jennifer got out of her daughter was that she had been involved with her 40-year-old French tutor and that as far as she knew he had gone back to Canada. Simon, it seemed, was the good-looking man with a Canadian accent whom Brian had sent packing when he found him and Debbie in a compromising clinch. Brian had needlessly feared the worse, and Debbie left home for a few days to cool off. It took some time for Debbie to recover from that incident.

WATER DOWN THE AM

But that was all water down the Am and long since forgotten. Debbie's relationship with Brian soon recovered and even grew stronger as they built up a working relationship. Then Simon Pemberton strode onto the scene – dark, handsome, complex and assured. His power fascinated Debbie while she tantalised him, and there was an instant attraction between the two, which Jennifer was quick to recognise.

A SMACK IN THE FACE

But her hopes for her daughter were dashed when Simon lost his temper and beat Debbie in a fit of frustrated rage. He tried to make amends but it was too late. In the meantime Brian was beside himself with fury and so over-protective of his step-daughter that Jennifer began to wonder whether another man would ever be allowed near her. The situation was resolved but in a way that no-one could have imagined. For Debbie's past was finally to catch up with her.

A BOLT FROM THE BLUE

Like a bolt from the blue, Simon Gerrard, her former tutor and lover, erupted back into her life. He arrived back in Borsetshire without any warning to work at a summer school, prior to taking up a post at Felpersham University. Debbie couldn't believe what was happening. She knew they were bound to meet again at some point, but eight years had gone by since she last saw him. What would he think of her now?

NO STRINGS

Debbie agreed to meet Simon, but this time it would have to be on her own terms. Simon would soon learn that she was very different from the young student he had left high and dry eight years ago, and certainly no longer 'tied to her mother's apron strings' as he had complained at the time. But the knowledge that he was back and might still care couldn't help but add a sparkle to Debbie's eyes, which Brian and Jennifer noticed with sinking hearts. Simon has been honest with Debbie. He knows he let her down badly back then, and that the timing was not right. Since then he's had another affair that went drastically wrong. 'It was all my fault,' he confessed. 'I'm screwed up when it comes to relationships.'

HOPES AND DOUBTS

Debbie was flattered that Simon's feelings led him to take a job in Felpersham, but if he's telling her the truth she can't understand why he didn't contact her beforehand. Maybe he was afraid of what her reaction might be, or didn't want to put pressure on her. But doubts trembled beneath the surface and Debbie resisted her instinctive desire to trust him.

RESISTANCE CRUMBLES

Then Simon asked for her help. He wanted to find a flat and he persuaded her to help him look for one. With a common goal in mind self-consciousness evaporated and it didn't take long for Debbie's resistance to crumble. She and Simon were back on the Ambridge map as an 'item'. This didn't please Brian and Jennifer at all, however

delighted they were that Debbie was happier than she had been for some time. Brian was furious that this was the man who had caused Debbie so much trouble in the past, and Jennifer was worried that he would let her down once again.

LOOKING FORWARD

As the academic year starts and Simon takes up his post at Felpersham University, which way will Debbie turn? She is now able to make decisions in her own right, but for once not even Debbie knows what is the best thing for her. Will she be content to stay in farming, or will she be tempted into a different way of life? In the meantime, Brian, for whom Debbie was the apple of his eye, keeps a stiff upper lip.

From left to right: *A family affair: Brian Aldridge with wife Jennifer and stepdaughter Debbie. Far right is Debbie's father and Jennifer's first husband, Roger Travers-Macy.*

THE PARGETTERS OF LOWER LOXLEY HALL

Like everyone else, the good folk of Ambridge are preparing to celebrate the New Millennium. Here are the millennium daydreams of some favourite Archers characters. First up: Nigel and Elizabeth Pargetter.

NIGEL   Don't you see Lizzie, this is a chance to get Lower Loxley back on a firm financial footing?

ELIZABETH   Yes, Nigel.

NIGEL   How about a three-day event, with some first-class astronomers? Let's see now, I wonder if Patrick Moore is free?

ELIZABETH   Good idea. We could set up a special exhibition — 'Paintings for the 21st century' — all at astronomical prices.

NIGEL   Yes, the commission would come in useful. And we mustn't forget publicity. I say, do we know anyone who's over a hundred?

ELIZABETH   You mean apart from Julia?

NIGEL   I do wish you would take this seriously, Lizzie. We could give them a slap-up dinner, get their photo in the papers — that sort of thing.

ELIZABETH   If you are asking me to be serious, Nigel, do you know what I'd really like?

NIGEL   No idea.

ELIZABETH   Well, just think how truly momentous it would be if this little bump of mine should decide to pop out for the New Millennium.

dreams...

NIGEL	Of course, Lizzie, darling. Even if we didn't plan it. It really would be something the Pargetter family hadn't done before.
JULIA	(APPROACH) What haven't the Pargetters done before?
NIGEL	We were just discussing the Millennium, Mummy, and Lizzie pointed out how wonderful it would be if the babies arrived at the turn of the century.
JULIA	Oh, that would be wonderful.
ELIZABETH	You really think so, Julia?
JULIA	(GOING) Certainly. I shall take charge of everything. You are not to worry. Twins should be no problem!
ELIZABETH	(OFF) The only problem is going to be Julia.
	(MUSIC)

WITH NO THEATRE OR CINEMA IN THE VILLAGE, THE RESIDENTS OF AMBRIDGE HAVE TO BE PRETTY SELF-RELIANT WHEN IT COMES TO ENTERTAINMENT. BUT, WITH AMBITIOUS LYNDA SNELL AND PROFESSIONAL LARRY LOVELL, THERE'S NEVER ANY SHORTAGE OF DRAMA FROM THE AMBRIDGE PLAYERS – BOTH ON AND OFF STAGE! HERE'S A LOOK BACK AT SOME PAST TRIUMPHS.

★ AMBRIDGE PLAYERS ★

proudly present their
Annual Christmas Pantomime
featuring
Characters you've never heard on radio!

JACK & THE BEANSTALK

with

Tracy Horrobin....as Jack
John Higgs....as Widow Twankey
Harry Roberts....as Mr Egg the Bailiff
Trudy Porter.....as Odorous Egg
Ivy Horrobin....as the Fairy

and featuring
Baggy and Snatch as Claribelle the Cow
The entire production directed by **Larry Lovell**

Ambridge Village Hall
29-31 December 1998

THE SHOW MUST GO ON

After a burst water pipe during the performance, a heroic front-of-house team saved the day. They battled manfully against disaster as the flood waters rose, threatening the vulnerable OAPs in the audience… Backstage crew stalwart to the last…

Effects and lighting would have done credit to Steven Spielberg. Magnificent musical accompaniment by Philip Archer.

Lynda Snell

A Midsummer
Night's Dream

**Ambridge Players' open-air production of
A Midsummer Night's Dream
by William Shakespeare**

**performed 3-5 September 1997
in the grounds of Lower Loxley Hall**

Titania......Elizabeth Pargetter
Hippolyta......Jill Archer
Hermia......Hayley Jordan
Helena......Kate Aldridge
Oberon......Nigel Pargetter
Puck......Rev Janet Fisher
Bottom......Eddie Grundy
Snout......Joe Grundy
Peter Quince......Bert Fry

Producer/director Lynda Snell
*whose extensive Shakespeare workshops ensured
the right casting for each character*

Borchester Echo

A rather avant-garde production. Special effects made the fairies even more magical, the illusion more enchanting and the dream even more surreal. Special mention must be made of the performances of Elizabeth and Nigel Pargetter who brought a touch of realism to the venomous arguments between proud Titania and jealous Oberon.

Larry Lovell

THE IMPORTANCE OF BEING EARNEST

by Oscar Wilde

AMBRIDGE VILLAGE HALL April 1990

Introducing the most audacious
performance ever seen on stage
Mrs Marjorie Antrobus as Lady Bracknell

The cast:

Lane, Merriman..........Bert Fry
Jack Worthing........Nelson Gabriel
Lady Bracknell......Marjorie Antrobus
Algernon.......Mark Hebden
Rev Canon Chasuble.......Jack Woolley
Miss Prism........Peggy Archer
Gwendoline.......Shula Hebden
Cecily Cardew.......Kathy Perks

Organised by **Elizabeth Archer** and **Lynda Snell**

A Lynda Snell Production

WILDE AT HEART

A truly audacious production! Marjorie Antrobus gave us Lady Bracknell as you've never seen her before. Excellent performance by Kathy Perks as a pert Cecily, and full marks to Nelson Gabriel who took over the part of Jack at the last moment. But Nelson, where did you find that wig? Bert Fry as the two manservants Lane and Merriman confused both himself and the audience as to which role he was playing.

Larry Lovell

fact file

NAME: MARJORIE ANTROBUS
BORN: 1922
ADDRESS: Nightingale Farm, Ambridge
OCCUPATION: Retired breeder and exhibitor of Afghan hounds
FAMILY: Widow of big game hunter, Teddy. No children
HOBBIES: Looking after her 'gels', the Afghans. Theatre Playing the organ
SINS: The occasional tipple

HIGHS

1985 Buys Nightingale Farm. At last: more room to breed Afghan hounds!

1989 Wins the Ambridge Spring Festival Talent Contest with Ruth Archer, singing 'Nice People with Nice Manners'

1999 Finds unexpected companionship when Hayley moves into the flat at Nightingale Farm.

LOWS

1987 Portia has a fling with Captain, Jack Woolley's bull terrier, and nine mongrel pups result.

1990 Turns down the opportunity to go on a missionary trip to Mozambique with Rev. Jerry Buckle, and is sad to lose a friend when he leaves.

1997 Has to leave her post as Official scorer for Ambridge Cricket Club after mistakes in the scoring.

1998 Fears she is going blind. Portia has to be put down.

What if...
Marjorie had gone on the stage professionally? She'd have been a sure-fire success, rival to Dame Judi Dench, and Ambridge would have lost her forever.

It's been a hard year for one of Ambridge's senior citizens, the much loved Marjorie Antrobus. She started to worry about her failing eyesight when she made errors scoring for the Ambridge Cricket Club, and was deeply embarrassed when, during the annual collection for the Poppy Appeal, she made a mistake on one of the forms. The error was put right and no harm was done, but Marjorie's troubles weren't over: just after this she was involved in a minor car accident. In fading light, Mrs Antrobus caught the wing of a passing car. Nothing serious, just broken wing mirrors – and fortunately the other party, Hayley Jordan, was most understanding. It was Hayley who took Mrs A (as she's affectionately known) to have her eyes tested, when it was discovered she needed a cataract operation. Relieved not to be going blind, Marjorie faces the operation with her usual stoicism.

As if this wasn't enough, Portia, one of Marjorie's Afghan hounds and a constant companion over the years, was taken ill and had to be put down. Hayley asked Marjorie if she could move into the vacant flat at Nightingale Farm. Marjorie was delighted to have a lodger again.

Marjorie has come a long way since her arrival in Ambridge in 1985. Until then she'd been living in a villa at Waterley Cross, but needed more room for breeding her Afghan hounds. When Nightingale Farm came on the market she thought she'd found the ideal home – but Ambridge folk are slow to accept newcomers, and it took some time before Marjorie, with the direct manners of a Colonial wife, met with approval. Joe Grundy dubbed her 'the dog woman' – a nickname that has stuck, but is now used with affection.

As Marjorie warmed to Ambridge, so Ambridge warmed to her, and it wasn't long before she could be seen sipping a glass of sherry in The Bull and chatting with other folk in the village shop. Although she has no children of her own, Marjorie has always had time for the young people of Ambridge and shown them a great deal of understanding.

On more than one occasion she has shown a talent for the theatre. Her performance as Lady Bracknell in *The Importance of Being Earnest* (1990) was described as 'superb', and she even won a prize in a talent contest, playing her electric organ and singing a Flanagan and Allen number with Ruth Archer.

Companionship, romantic or otherwise, continues to elude Marjorie. She was attracted to the military dash of Colonel Danby – reminded, perhaps, of her late husband Teddy – but the relationship never got off the ground. Her soft spot for Guy Pemberton developed into a mild flirtation, but then he married Caroline. Once Marjorie plucked up the courage to answer a lonely hearts advertisement in the *Borchester Echo* – only to find out that the lonely heart in question belonged to Joe Grundy.

A devout Christian, always willing to help other people, Marjorie Antrobus is valued by the community she serves so well, but remains lonely. Her friendship with Hayley may make all the difference.

Margot Boyd

How much of Margot Boyd is there in Marjorie Antrobus? She's certainly got the theatrical flair: Margot fell in love with the stage during regular visits to the Old Vic during its pre-war glory days, and decided to pursue an acting career by training at RADA. She paid her dues in twice-nightly rep at the Theatre Royal, Leeds, before graduating to seasons at Stratford and a starring role in Noël Coward's *Waiting in the Wings*. She got her radio training as a stalwart of the BBC Drama Repertory Company – and from there it was a short, natural step to Ambridge.

The rest of the character, though, is based on observation. Margot modelled Mrs A on women that she met in Somerset, where her father managed a large estate, and on the dog breeders that she has observed over years of regular visits to Crufts. As for Mrs Antrobus's warm heart and friendly understanding – that, say colleagues on *The Archers*, comes directly from Margot Boyd herself.

BROOKFIELD:
TIME FOR CHANGE?

For decades, Brookfield has represented a kind of rural ideal, the traditional English mixed farm. But now, Phil Archer is handing over the reins to his son David, and a new era is about to begin. Can Brookfield survive and flourish into the next Millennium?

There have always been Archers at Brookfield – at least since 1917, when Dan succeeded to the tenancy. Over the years, the farm has developed to meet the demands of modern farming, but now it's facing one of the biggest challenges in its history as Dan's grandson David takes over from his father, Phil. There are all the day-to-day problems to contend with as well as the responsibility for taking Brookfield forward. David and Ruth will, like many farmers, consider how to manage in the future with fewer subsidies, plus the merits of the proposed lambing co-operative – but as we reach the end of the twentieth century there are bigger issues at stake. Farming is in deep crisis. World prices for beef, lamb and pork are at rock bottom; supermarkets are forcing payments to farmers down while keeping prices high in the shops. If David and Ruth are going to make a go of Brookfield and keep the farm intact to hand on to their children Pip and Josh, they're going to have to achieve little short of a miracle.

For nearly 50 years British farmers have looked to *The Archers* for a reflection of the real issues facing them, and it would be unreal if David and Ruth were immune to the general problems. But David, at least, is an optimist: 'I know that global markets are volatile,' he says, 'but I reckon that farm prices will bottom out and 2000 will bring them back to a reasonable level.' And things could be a lot worse: just down the road, the Grundys are in much bigger trouble.

David and Ruth can't wait to put their ideas into action. It hasn't all been plain sailing. They have been keen to take charge for a long time, but it's only Jill's broken kneecap that's finally led to Phil taking more of a back seat. Brookfield has often been the scene of heated father and son disagreements, first between Dan and Phil and more recently between Phil and David, over how the farm should develop. The rows were upsetting but they often produced useful solutions to the farming problems under discussion. Phil is still be there to consult when necessary, but the real responsibility lies with David and Ruth. They're full of ideas, eager to reassess their situation and count their assets, planning for a brighter future. It can't be any worse than the last two years!

Whatever the outcome, one thing's for sure: Brookfield will continue to mirror the real experience of many British farmers.

Phil took over from his father Dan in 1969

Phil and Jill will still keep an eye on Brookfield

LIFE IMITATES ART

- Brookfield has always been the centre of farming activities in Ambridge. It was the farm around which everything revolved when *The Archers* began back in 1951, following the farmers' cry of 'What we need is an agricultural Dick Barton!'

- Editor Godfrey Baseley seized the opportunity to introduce farmers to modern methods and technology. It wasn't long before farmers were saying 'If Dan Archer's doing that at Brookfield, we'd better do it'.

- Not that *The Archers* was ever a nice re-hash of Ministry of Agriculture pamphlets. Soon Dan was heard on Budget Day discussing with Phil what the Chancellor's proposals would mean to farmers.

How it was: Phil, Doris, Dan and Christine take breakfast in the Brookfield kitchen

BROOKFIELD TIGHTENS ITS BELT

The days when Dan Archer kept a team of farm workers have long gone. Now it's David and Ruth who do the lion's share of the manual work on the farm, helped by Bert Fry, and Phil lends a hand as often as his son will allow. For the rest David brings in specialised machinery, and employs casual labour as and when required. Only last year pigman Harry Roberts had to be made redundant as an economy measure.

Economy has been the watchword at Brookfield over the last 12 months. When a farm is run this efficiently there's so little fat to trim that many of the economies have had to be domestic. Ruth has risen to the challenge with her usual energy and has all sorts of good ideas for saving, buying children's clothes second-hand and growing her own vegetables in the little spare time she has. This year she'll try and make time to keep the farm books up to date, and so reduce the accountant's charges.

David's doing his bit too. He made the supreme sacrifice of selling his expensive four-wheel-drive vehicle, although he could hardly do less as Ruth was combing Borchester's second-hand shops to find winter clothes for the children. Of course, no-one wants to economise on the children, but as David points out, in hard times everyone has to shoulder their share of the burden.

There is such a thing as false economy, as Ruth and David have learned to their cost. When they started to change the cows' bedding less frequently than usual, they ran into trouble; one cow soon needed attention from the vet, who told them to clean out the bedding area at least once a month or run the risk of all the cows becoming infected. As Bert Fry told them, with typical country wisdom, 'Even Eddie Grundy knows that baler twine is a poor substitute for a properly repaired fence when it comes to keeping sheep in their place.' Bert's trust in Eddie may be misplaced but David and Ruth certainly got the message!

BROOKFIELD DISASTERS

- Dan lost his main crop of potatoes to blight, a barn fire destroyed a field of oats, lambs were killed when lightning struck a tree and free range hens succumbed to fowl pest.

- The biggest disaster was in 1956, shortly after Dan had acquired the freehold of Brookfield, when all his cattle and sheep had to be destroyed because of an outbreak of foot-and-mouth disease. Phil and Jill agree that this was far worse than their 1998 outbreak of TB when a hefty proportion of the herd was slaughtered.

- Not all the problems at Brookfield have been due to natural disasters. The dairy herd had to be cut back on the introduction of milk quotas, and in 1986 Phil had to sell off 55 acres in order to pay death duties.

The new breed: David and Ruth have big ideas for Brookfield

DRAMAS AND FARMERS

Agricultural story editor Graham Harvey
has to make sure that The Archers reflects reality

Much as I love *The Archers* I never expected to die for the series. But the day I acted as catcher for a trio of professional sheep shearers it began to feel as if I might.

It had all seemed such a great idea in theory – getting the flavour of a truly demanding farm task. The catcher's role is to grab a ewe from out of the bunch and drag her to the shearing stand, then go back for the next one.

Sounds easy enough, I thought. A few hours of this and I'll be able to give the writers a true picture of this annual event, just the way they do it at Home Farm or Brookfield. What I didn't realise was you have to be fit enough for Gladiators to last more than half an hour.

My three shearers were getting each ewe clipped in an average of a minute and a half, which meant that to keep them busy I had to wrestle a reluctant sheep from pen to shearing point in no more than half a minute. Any longer and I'd be holding them up. More important, I'd be losing them money.

After an hour of this I'd started hurting in places I never knew I had muscles. After two hours I was ready for intensive care. Somehow I managed to survive – but the next time I come across a mention of sheep shearing in a script I'll be expecting at least a passing reference to the sheer, unadulterated pain of the job.

Maintaining close links with day-to-day practical farming is important in keeping the drama fresh and authentic. The scriptwriters have their own personal contacts in the farming community; they've found that a brief phone conversation with a farmer can help them bring freshness and energy to a working scene. Spiced with the kind of anecdote that only a real countryman can provide, the scene takes on a new vitality. It becomes like a real slice of country life.

But the job of putting farming and the countryside at the heart of this rural drama begins long before the writers start penning dialogue. My first task as agricultural story editor is to provide the writers with a set of farming notes covering the month they're about to write. It'll outline the chief activities on our four featured farms. For example, the notes for late May are likely to tell the writers that they're making silage at Brookfield, while at Home Farm Debbie is spraying wheat crops against fungal disease. The writers can use such seasonal details in their dialogue. They can also set scenes in work situations, thus creating the atmosphere of a busy working farm.

The other key element of my job is to devise storylines that will keep farming and countryside matters right at the heart of *The Archers*. For this I rely on a variety of news sources to keep me up-to-date – the farming press, Radio 4's *Farming Today* and, increasingly, the general and consumer press which now run regular features on farming and food issues.

But while we try to be contemporary in covering matters of current concern, we don't let issues lead the drama. The days when new farming developments came over almost as official announcements are long gone.

Rather we think about how such developments will affect our characters, then devise stories that will explore this in a dramatic and naturalistic way. Instead of explaining farming's current economic crisis in dialogue, for example, we follow the stresses and strains that financial hardship puts on any family. Clarrie Grundy comes close to despair in trying to make ends meet, while at Brookfield the need to economise produces a rift between the generations.

Farming and countryside matters will remain centre stage in *The Archers*. But we won't mind if listeners hardly notice. We're hoping they'll be too absorbed in the drama.

IT HAPPENED HERE

Look behind any hedgerow, open any barn door in Ambridge and you're sure to find some kind of drama unfolding. Here's a handy at-a-glance guide to who's done what to whom – and where!

Dower House

Heydon Berrow

Red H

HEYDON BERROW

A rare black woodpecker makes its first UK appearance! George Barford and William Grundy are the first to spot it, but when news gets out, the area is besieged by twitchers. Understandably, the woodpecker flies away. Bye bye birdie, bye bye twitchers.

Valley Farm

Heydon Farm

Brookfield

Heydon Brook

Bungalow

Sawyer's Farm
(Estate Office)

Ambridge Hall

April

HOME FARM

Bealtech's trial plot of genetically modified oilseed rape is attacked. The crop is resistant to herbicide, but can't stand sickles. David Archer is a witness, and Tommy Archer one of the gang.

LEADERS WOOD

William Grundy found wild boar hoofprints; the boar found the Gloucester Old Spot sow; she found she had five strange piglets; Tommy Archer found that boar piglets make exceedingly good sausages.

Home Farm

How to spot an
Archers Addict

Worried about a family member, friend or neighbour? Do th[ey stay]
indoors glued to the radio? Do they talk with inappropri[ate]
about milk yield and bovine TB? They may be an Archers [addict, so]
follow this simple checklist to be sure, then try and get the p[erson to do a]
quiz on page 90 to find out just how bad the problem is.

AN ARCHERS ADDICT:

Has a need to be involved in other people's problems and affairs

Lives in a town, but hankers after living in the country

Has an interest in farming, but not all that mucking-out stuff

Would like to be friends with the Grundys, as long as they don't come too close

Has lots of *Archers* stories which begin: 'Do you remember when. . .'

Can tell you the names of all the *Archers* characters since 1951,
and who played them

Never watches *Coronation Street*

Has a small but treasured collection of *Archers* memorabilia

Phones in for a ticket as soon as any *Archers* event is announced

Can tell you where both The Bull and St Stephen's church are situated

Has a photographic memory of the map of Ambridge

Reads both *Ambridge Village Voice* and the *Borchester Echo* from cover to cover
the day they arrive

Owns mugs with 'dum di dum di dum di dum' printed on them

Won't make arrangements on Sunday mornings

Knows all the words of 'The Village Pump'

Says 'Aaaah' at the end of each episode

Never wears green wellies

Knows the current price of a pint of Shires in The Bull

Lists the birthdays of all the *Archers* characters in their diary

Now turn to page 90 to find out more. . .

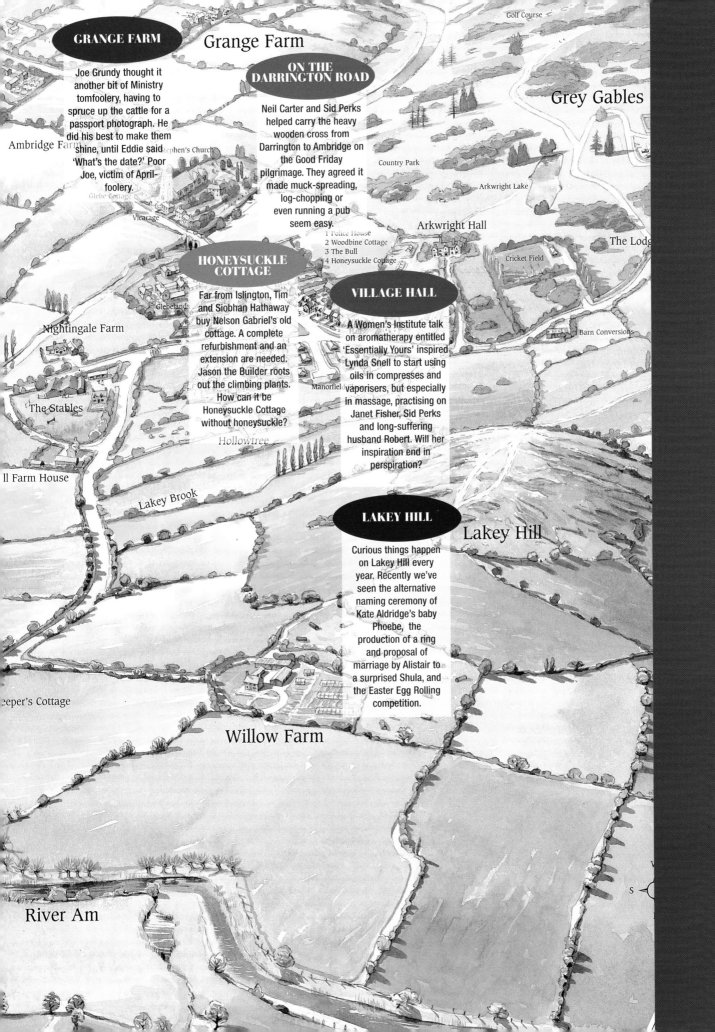

Golf Course

Grange Farm

Grey Gables

GRANGE FARM

Joe Grundy thought it another bit of Ministry tomfoolery, having to spruce up the cattle for a passport photograph. He did his best to make them shine, until Eddie said 'What's the date?' Poor Joe, victim of April-foolery.

ON THE DARRINGTON ROAD

Neil Carter and Sid Perks helped carry the heavy wooden cross from Darrington to Ambridge on the Good Friday pilgrimage. They agreed it made muck-spreading, log-chopping or even running a pub seem easy.

Country Park

Arkwright Lake

Arkwright Hall

The Lodge

Ambridge Farm

Stephen's Church

Glebe Cottage

Vicarage

1 Police House
2 Woodbine Cottage
3 The Bull
4 Honeysuckle Cottage

Cricket Field

HONEYSUCKLE COTTAGE

Far from Islington, Tim and Siobhan Hathaway buy Nelson Gabriel's old cottage. A complete refurbishment and an extension are needed. Jason the Builder roots out the climbing plants. How can it be Honeysuckle Cottage without honeysuckle?

Glebelands

VILLAGE HALL

A Women's Institute talk on aromatherapy entitled 'Essentially Yours' inspired Lynda Snell to start using oils in compresses and vaporisers, but especially in massage, practising on Janet Fisher, Sid Perks and long-suffering husband Robert. Will her inspiration end in perspiration?

Barn Conversions

Nightingale Farm

Hall

Manorfield

The Stables

Hollowtree

Lakey Brook

ll Farm House

LAKEY HILL

Curious things happen on Lakey Hill every year. Recently we've seen the alternative naming ceremony of Kate Aldridge's baby Phoebe, the production of a ring and proposal of marriage by Alistair to a surprised Shula, and the Easter Egg Rolling competition.

Lakey Hill

eeper's Cottage

Willow Farm

River Am

S

ANNUAL!

Number 3476 Winter 2000

SHULA HEBDEN LLOYD, WHO CAUSED SO MUCH SCANDAL IN AMBRIDGE LAST YEAR, REVEALS HER INNERMOST THOUGHTS TO ANNUAL! READERS

THE SHULA HEBDEN LLOYD INTERVIEW

HAPPY START TO A LIFE MARKED BY TRAGEDY

Shula becomes Mrs Mark Hebden, while Lord Lichfield (extreme right) captures the moment for her wedding album

Shula Hebden Lloyd lives in a charmingly thatched cottage next to St Stephen's Church. She has money and looks, is very much in love with her husband, vet Alistair Lloyd, and is proud mother of Daniel (aged five) by her first husband, Mark Hebden. She runs a riding school with her aunt, Christine Barford.

Someone who has everything, you might say. But when you scratch the surface there is far more to this vulnerable, courageous woman than is immediately obvious.

Shula, many people move away from where they were brought up. Yet you, your brother David and sister Elizabeth have all stayed in or near Ambridge. Why do you think this is?
I suppose we're just a family of home-lovers! The Archers have farmed at Brookfield for generations and David's just taken over from Dad, who is now semi-retired. And Elizabeth married Nigel Pargetter who owns Lower Loxley Hall which she helps him run as a conference centre. So there are practical reasons why they've never moved.

And you?
There have been times when I've thought about moving, but to be honest I can't imagine living anywhere else. We are an incredibly close family and they mean everything to me. All my friends are here too. What would be the point of moving?

What about your social life as you grew up. Did you have one?
I certainly did! It was quite lively I can tell you, and I thought I was very sophisticated – especially when I went out with Simon Parker. He was a

journalist on the *Borchester Echo* at the time and I was very impressed.

And why was he so special?

Let's just say he was my first real relationship. We shared an unrepeatable moment. He was very very naughty! Looking back I feel really sorry for Mum and Dad. I had all sorts of boyfriends, none of them what you might call suitable, and they didn't like any of them much. The worst was a chap called Nick Wearing, who left me on my own in Bangkok with no passport and no belongings. I thought I'd never see Ambridge again. It was such an awful experience that I really had to take stock of myself and my love life. I suppose Mark turned up at just the right time.

Mark Hebden – up and coming young solicitor?

Yes. I can't believe that I actually broke off our first engagement, wasting all that precious time. He nearly married someone else but fortunately I came to my senses.

CLOUDS ON THE HORIZON

Shula and Mark's marriage was one of the highlights in the Social Diary of 1985. They were married at St Stephen's, with the reception at Netherbourne Hall (Lord Lichfield took the photographs) and the bride looked enchanting. The couple soon settled into their respective roles as lawyer and land agent.

But there was one cloud on the horizon. They both very much wanted to have a child, but it was five years before Shula became pregnant. Sadly it was an ectopic pregnancy which had to be terminated.

How did you feel?

Everyone kept telling me it was nobody's fault and rationally I knew they were right but I couldn't help feeling that I'd let Mark down. I had all sorts of tests and medical checks which just went on and on, but in the end *in vitro* fertilisation treatment seemed our only hope. That didn't seem to be working either but at least

Shula's first husband Mark Hebden turned up 'just at the right time'

Simon Pemberton, scourge of the women of Ambridge

'I still don't find it easy to talk about this time in my life'

Mark and I were able to talk about it and in a peculiar way we were closer than we'd been for a long time.

Then Mark died in a tragic accident?
Yes. I was actually talking to him on his mobile phone only seconds before he swerved to avoid my good friend Caroline Pemberton on her horse. He crashed and died instantly. There's not a lot to say. I still don't find it easy to talk about this time in my life.

And then you discovered you were pregnant again?
It was very strange. I was in mourning but I was creating a new life. I wanted to die myself but I had everything to live for. In the end of course Daniel brought back meaning to my life. I had to keep going even when I wanted most to give in.

NEW LOVES, HARD LESSONS

They say that it takes two years to recover from a traumatic experience. Was that true for you?
Yes, I think that's probably right. I was working at Rodway and Watson, the estate agents, and about two years after Mark died, I started going out with one of their clients, Simon Pemberton. Simon seemed so strong and sure and was very good with Daniel and I started to fall in love with him. Although I knew he could be ruthless he was never like that with me, and it was only when I discovered that he was seeing someone else and lying to me that we quarrelled. And he actually hit me.

I still don't really know why I reacted as I did – keeping it from everyone as though I had something to be ashamed of and not him! Crazy! He tried to patch it up but I had the sense to say no. Then he went out with Debbie Aldridge, my second cousin, and I found out he actually beat up Debbie. I was mortified that my silence led to her injuries. We talked about it and decided we should put a stop to it, so she took him to court and I was a witness against him.

You must have felt very exposed?
Very. But it had to be done.

But worse was to come?
Yes. I got into a terrible mess and became the talk of the village. Daniel was ill and I was desperately worried. Our doctor, Richard Locke, lived with Usha Gupta who had been Mark's business partner and was a family friend, so I knew him well. He was very easy to talk to. Richard seemed to take a personal interest in us and after all the lonely times it was heaven to have someone who really cared about Daniel and me.

We became closer and closer until inevitably we found ourselves in bed together. I felt ashamed, ecstatic, alive and terrified. I knew what I was doing but I couldn't seem to stop myself, and the worst of it is that quite apart from deceiving Usha I was also seeing Alistair! I'd like to think it was a big reaction to all that had happened to me – nothing to do with the real me at all. I know, truthfully, that there are no excuses for what Simon did to me or what I did to Usha. You wish you could rewind the tape and make everything better, but sadly it's just not possible.

So what happened?
It all came out in the end, of course. It had to. Usha was hurt and furious,

> **'There are no excuses for what Simon did to me or what I did to Usha. You wish you could rewind the tape and make everything better, but sadly it's just not possible'**

Dishy Doc Locke prescribes fresh air and exercise!

'I know how lucky I am'

Shula and Daniel: happy at last

my parents couldn't understand what was going on, Alistair was disgusted with me, the family started taking sides, and I knew all the villagers were talking about me behind my back. If anyone reading this is tempted to do the same, all I can say is *stop*. Now. It can never be worth it.

And what did you do?

Richard wanted me to leave Ambridge and go to Manchester with him. But I couldn't imagine uprooting Daniel, or myself for that matter. I realised that I was attracted to the fact that he reassured me at a time when I desperately needed it, as much as I was to Richard himself. And, of course, there was Alistair.

HAPPY EVER AFTER?

When did you and Alistair get back together?

After Richard left I realised just how much I cared for Alistair but I didn't know what to do about it. I suggested meeting, having a drink or a meal, but just came up against this wall of polite rejection. David told me to keep trying but it was one of the receptionists at the surgery, Susan Carter, who tipped the balance in the end.

We were at a Cricket Club meeting and, in front of everyone, she said something about knowing why Richard had left so suddenly. I couldn't bear it. I rushed away and Alistair came after me, mopped up my tears and told me he loved me. We got engaged pretty soon afterwards and were married on Christmas Eve last year.

Has it been worth it?

Forgiving myself has been hard but Alistair has helped enormously. I've had bad times but I've put them behind me. I have Daniel and Alistair and good friends, and I work in a job I love. I know how lucky I am.

fact file

NAME: KATHERINE (KATE) VICTORIA ALDRIDGE
BORN: 30 September 1977
ADDRESS: Home Farm, Ambridge
OCCUPATION: Mainly idle. Helps out occasionally at village shop
FAMILY: A daughter, Phoebe
HOBBIES: Alternative medicine, swimming, vegetarian cookery, the environment, pagan rituals
SINS: Smokes illegal substances, known by Borsetshire Constabulary, tendency to disappear without telling anyone where she's going

HIGHS

1988 Delighted when her parents are asked to remove her from Cheltenham Ladies College. Anticipates greater freedom at home for boyfriends and body piercing.

1991 Enjoys being leader of the Blossom Hill Cottage Gang. Writes to Peggy Woolley's old wartime flame, Conn Kortchmar, and is thrilled when he comes over to claim Peggy!

1994 Runs away to join new-age travellers rather than re-sit GCSEs at Borchester College. Doesn't re-establish contact with her family for months.

1998 Gives birth to her daughter in a tepee at Glastonbury, attended only by Morwenna her midwife friend – just as she wanted.

LOWS

1991 Attends family therapy sessions on sufferance with her mother – a complete waste of time.

1993 Scared when there is a raid on the village shop. Acts like a heroine and lets down the tyres of the getaway van.

1995 Frightened when she is rushed into hospital after mixing temazepam and alcohol.

1998 Annoyed by Roy Tucker's insistence on paternity rights. Grudgingly gives access to see Phoebe from time to time.

What Kate didn't know...

Phoebe is an old family name. Kate's great great grandmother, wife of John Archer (Dan's father) was called Phoebe.

Has motherhood helped Kate to settle down and become a more responsible caring individual, or is she biding her time ready to dash off to the next protest, with Phoebe under one arm and a banner under the other?

Every village has one, as do many families – a girl who, despite being given the best opportunities in life, decides to thumb her nose at authority and kick over the traces. Where, everyone wonders, did it all go wrong?

In Ambridge, it's Kate Aldridge, 22-year-old daughter of Brian and Jennifer Aldridge. She was born in 1977 and educated at Cheltenham Ladies College, Borchester Green School, Borchester Tech – and later at Scandals Bar in Borchester, at festivals up and down the country, and in a protest tree camp on the Borchester by-pass. If there's trouble anywhere Kate is sure to be up to her neck in it.

Kate decamped after receiving her disappointing GCSE results, lived in various squats and acquired some highly undesirable companions. Inevitably this caused a great deal of heartache for the bemused Brian and Jennifer.

Eventually Kate returned home and with Roy borrowed enough money from her grandmother, Peggy Woolley, to buy a mobile catering van to cook and serve vegetarian food at summer festivals.

Her actions aroused some disapproval but she found support from unlikely people such as Lynda Snell, with whom she could talk through her troubles. Even Jack Woolley helped out when he gave her a job in the village shop.

Encouraged by her new-age friends, Kate – always ready for a fight – quickly developed a taste for environmental protest. When she organised a camp against the widening of the Borchester by-pass, she was arrested. Brian and Jennifer had the ignominy of collecting their unrepentant daughter from the police station.

Then came the shocking news. Kate was pregnant, but refused to name the father. Was it Luther, whom she'd got to know on the road? Or milkman's son Roy Tucker?

Worse followed when, in the last stages of pregnancy, Kate took off again, and gave birth not in a hospital but in a tepee at the Glastonbury Festival. When she got home she infuriated everyone by calling the infant 'baby' for months. Once Roy Tucker proved he was the father, he insisted upon his rights, and Kate had to give in or face a difficult and protracted court case. She initially agreed to limited contact time, but soon found that a willing father makes an excellent baby-sitter.

Baby Phoebe is now delighting the family as she starts to walk and talk. The Aldridges are getting used to sharing her with her other grandparents, Betty and Mike Tucker. But one thing's for sure: no one knows what Kate will do next.

Kellie Bright

Like many girls, Kellie Bright always wanted to be a dancer, and got her foot on the ladder at the age of eight, playing the title role in an amateur production of *Annie*.

After that there was no looking back. Kellie went to drama school, and at nine landed the role of Young Cosette in *Les Misérables* in the West End. Two years later she was playing children's roles on television, went on to appear in pantomime, and after an audition was offered the part of the rebellious Kate Aldridge in *The Archers*.

Kellie sees the part as a reflection of a huge number of contemporary young people, and as a warning to parents of the danger signs to watch out for. Will Kate ever turn from her rebellious ways? Kellie suspects she may do, 'but not yet'.

Jennifer's Diary

A lot can happen in a year in Ambridge. Thank goodness someone's been keeping a note of things! Here's a chance to remember a few highlights of 1999 with a sneak peek into my diary. . .

JANUARY 1999

I've spotted Susan Carter going into Lower Loxley several times. Rumour has it Julia is writing a racy novel and dictating à la Barbara Cartland to Susan to help pay off her Spanish debts. Can't wait to read it.

Hayley Jordan is moving into Nightingale Farm. Just the tonic Marjorie Antrobus needs. She's been really depressed since Portia was put down.

Kate's helping out at the Village Shop so I get to baby-sit Phoebe, which is great fun.

Debbie says young William Grundy is a natural with animals. He wants to be a gamekeeper. Better than hanging round street corners.

FEBRUARY 1999

I liked Helen's designs for the new Bridge Farm logo. Should help put their produce on the map.

Mum thought Tommy and Hayley's leek and pork sausages were delicious but Pat and Tony won't let her help fund them. Trouble brewing there, I'm afraid.

Dr Tim Hathaway has arrived from London. People say he's dishy so I'm looking forward to meeting him.

Popped into The Bull to find out about Comic Relief night. Sid was actually practising with his dumb-bells behind the bar while serving! Later I heard he'd dropped them on his foot and been rushed to hospital. So much for keep fit.

MARCH 1999

They're lambing at Brookfield so it's all hands to the pump. Jill's looking tired. She's doing the school run with Pip, as well as looking after Josh, and Daniel when he's not at nursery school. Where would they all be without us grannies to pick up the pieces when we're needed?

The Grundys can't find the rent (surprise, surprise!) and want time to pay. Of course Brian's sympathetic but Borchester Land won't wear it. They'll have to find some money pretty smartly or they'll be in trouble.

Daniel's being a pain. Alistair's very patient with him and I'm sure it'll sort itself out in the end. But aren't children difficult!

I like the idea of the monthly Farmers' Market in Borchester. Should be able to buy some rather interesting breads and cheeses – always good for impressing Brian's friends at our little dinner parties. Jill wants to sell her free range eggs and home-made honey and jams and I expect Mike and Neil will be there in June with their strawberries. Jolly good.

APRIL 1999

Pat's very down. Still missing John. Tony's had to call the doctor and he's put her on medication.

Helen's in charge of the dairy. She's promoted Tracy Horrobin to temporary supervisor, which she may live to regret.

The architect has given a thumbs up to Elizabeth's idea of converting one of the barns at Lower Loxley into an art gallery and bistro. Rather fun.

Jason has started building a new extension for Dr Tim and Siobhan Hathaway at Honeysuckle Cottage. I wonder what dear old Walter would have said about that!

MAY 1999

It's absolutely outrageous. All Brian is doing is exploring possibilities with his GM trial crop, and the village organises a protest meeting! Large turn-out. Tony's no help.

Then David and Ruth caught a gang of vandals attacking the crop with sickles. Brian's had to get the police in. (I'm surprised anyone knows how to use a sickle these days.)

The dreaded Julia has paid off her debt to Ronald Hardwicke. She's been staying with her daughter Camilla who's given her the money. Anything to get rid of her!

George is to be the new Ambridge Tree Warden. Christine's really pleased.

The Rev Janet is training hard for her Third World Debt March to Cologne. Usha plans to go part of the way with her. Beats me how two so-called professional ladies can just down tools and go off. What happens to Janet's parishioners, and Usha's clients?

I've just heard that Tommy might be one of the gang involved in the sickle-attack on the GM rape crop, and has been taken to court. Oh dear; this will be the last straw for poor Pat. I do feel for her.

JUNE 1999

Jill has hurt her knee quite badly. David and Ruth have moved into Brookfield and Phil and Jill are at the bungalow, so she can get about more easily.

The walkers return – Janet went the full distance to Cologne, all 405 miles in just 19 days and, despite huge blisters, had a marvellous time. Rather her than me!

Lovely news. Lizzie is expecting. She's feeling a bit sick – only natural. Nigel is so excited, and of course Jill will have time to knit those lovely little matinée jackets.

JULY 1999

Simon Gerrard, that awful French lecturer at Exeter, who was responsible for Debbie dropping out has suddenly turned up. I just came across the pair of them chatting away like old friends! What on earth does the man think he's doing?

Jolene Rogers is starting up her line-dancing classes at The Bull again. Perhaps Brian and I should sign up. I wonder if there's still anything between Jolene and Eddie Grundy. If I were Clarrie, I'd worry with a woman like that on the scene. On second thoughts, perhaps we'll give the classes a miss...

AUGUST 1999

Brian really is his own worst enemy. If he carries on like this, he's going to drive Debbie out of the house. He's right that Simon is much older than Debbie, but no man will ever match up to what Brian wants for her. As for me, of course I'm worried. I just want Debbie to be happy and if this is what she wants, well... Oh dear, why is love so complicated?

I despair of the Grundys. Eddie has just tried to get away with some ridiculous axe-throwing stunt at the fête, all for a paltry £25. Well, now he's got a van window to replace, too. It's lucky someone wasn't injured.

SEPTEMBER 1999

I have to say that I think I may have been wrong about Simon. He really is a most charming man, and he and Debbie seem genuinely fond of each other. Brian can't see it, of course. He seems to think that Simon is some kind of gold-digger. He's behaving very strangely about the whole affair.

Saw Janet Fisher in the churchyard. Seems the trip to Cologne has given her itchy feet. I hope we're not going to lose her. She's such a sane person. Poor Mrs Antrobus is still waiting to have her cataracts done. She's lucky she's got Hayley to look after her.

OCTOBER 1999

Debbie has moved in with Simon, and it's all Brian's fault! I warned him this would happen if he carried on the way he was. I was starting to look forward to Christmas and the new millennium. Now what will the future bring?

Christmas Recipes

Christmas is coming, and all over Ambridge kitchens are abuzz with preparations for the big day. Here are three festive recipes that make the holiday season go with a swing!

Phil really enjoys gathering his grandchildren around him to get them cooking. Here is an easy recipe for Christmas that Pip and Daniel can make under supervision. Josh is allowed to sprinkle them with sugar when they are cooked! They all help Phil decorate the tree.

Phil's Festive Almond Biscuits

Put the butter in a food processor with the flour and almonds. Whizz to fine breadcrumbs. Add half the caster sugar; whizz until the mixture starts to cling together, then work lightly into a ball with your hands. Thinly roll out half of the dough between two pieces of plastic film on a lightly floured surface. Use a 6cm/2½in cutter to cut out crescents; put 10 on a greased baking sheet. Roll half the marzipan into sausages and lay on the crescents. Top each with another crescent (reroll trimmings if necessary) and seal the edges.

Make stars with remaining dough and marzipan. Chill for 30 minutes. Preheat the oven to 160C/Gas 3/fan oven 150C. Pare strips of orange rind, put on a baking sheet and bake for 3 minutes to dry out slightly; cool. Mix the remaining caster sugar and the icing sugar; toss with the rind. Bake biscuits for 18 – 20 minutes; cool on a wire rack. Gently toss in a little of the orange sugar and pack; sprinkle with the remaining sugar.

These will keep in an airtight container for 1 week, so make a day or so ahead.

Ingredients

Preparation 30 minutes
Cooking 20 minutes
Makes 20

75g/3oz unsalted butter, chilled and cut into pieces
115g/4oz self-raising flour
75g/3oz ground almonds
100g/4oz caster sugar
50g/2oz marzipan, cut into 20 cubes
2 oranges
50g/2oz icing sugar

Grey Gables Goose

Remove the giblets and use them to make a stock. Cover with water and half a glass of red wine, add one onion roughly chopped, a carrot or some celery. Season to taste, bring to the boil and simmer for an hour.

Fill the tail end of the bird with the stuffing and secure the gap with a small skewer.

Loosely wrap foil round the wings and the legs. Prick the fleshy parts with a skewer and dust all over with seasoned flour.

Place the goose directly onto the centre rack of a pre-heated oven ensuring that a roasting tray lies at the base of the oven to collect the fat. Cook at gas mark 7, 425F, 220C for the first half hour, then lower the temperature to gas mark 4, 350F, 180C for a further three hours. If it cooks faster than you imagined, don't worry – the goose can rest for up to half an hour without losing heat. You may need to empty the tray once or twice, so have a large bowl to hand to pour the fat into. (You'll have enough goose dripping to cook crisp roast potatoes all the way through till Easter!)

When ready, remove foil, lift out of the oven and slip onto a large, hot serving dish. Make some gravy with a little fat, some of the pan juices and the giblet stock. Serve with roast potatoes and apple wedges.

'C'est magnifique! You will never forget this experience!' says Jean-Paul.

When Jean-Paul is asked for an alternative to the more traditional roast turkey a reverential look comes into his eyes, he snaps his fingers and exclaims 'But of course! Bien sur! We will have the most delicious goose with tender flesh and crispy brown skin, accompanied by my fantastic stuffing – naturellement!' And that's the last we see of him for some time.

Ingredients

One goose with giblets weighing 12lb/5.5kg will serve eight people
Seasoned flour
2 cox's apples, cut into wedges and lightly fried, to serve
A sprig of rosemary to garnish

For the Stuffing Fantastique

6 large cox's apples peeled, cored and chopped
4 tablespoons dark rum
1 teaspoon chopped fresh sage leaves
1 teaspoon grated nutmeg
Fine grated rind of one orange
12oz/350g fresh breadcrumbs
Seasoning to taste

Soak the apple in the rum (Jean-Paul suggests you test quality of the rum first) for three hours.

Add the remaining ingredients and mix well.

Freda Fry's Heart Warming Soup for the Carol Singers

Traditionally, when the carol singers arrive at Woodbine Cottage their hearts lift: they know that after they have sung Bert and Freda's favourite carol, 'God Rest Ye Merry Gentlemen', they will each be given a steaming mug of Freda's warming Broccoli and Stilton Soup. Freda has kindly shared the recipe.

Ingredients

1 large peeled onion
6oz/150g peeled potato
1 tbsp olive oil
1lb/450g broccoli
1½pt/850ml chicken stock
6oz/150g finely chopped Stilton cheese
Salt and pepper
Chopped fresh tarragon and parsley to garnish

Chop the onion and potato into small pieces and fry gently in the oil.

Trim the broccoli, and cut the florets (including stems) into small slices. Add to the onion and potato, season well and fry for five minutes. Add the stock and simmer for 20 minutes.

Put the soup into a liquidiser or food processor and blend. Pour into mugs, sprinkle with finely chopped Stilton, stirring with a spoon until the cheese has melted into the soup. Garnish with the chopped herbs.

Just what the Ambridge carol singers need on a cold and frosty night!

THE CARTERS AT NO. 1 THE GREEN

Susan Carter's dream is no secret. Born a Horrobin, she wants to get away from her working class roots, to escape the Horrobin hex. Her biggest wish for the Millennium is for Neil to give up his job as farm worker and handyman, and return to being a sales rep for Borchester Mills.

She'd shine his shoes, buy him a new suit, a dazzling white shirt and discreet tie. Then, in her best dress, all accessories matching, hair carefully styled, she would accompany him to the office party. As she sips dry white wine and giggles with the other wives, she watches proudly as Neil buys a round for his white-collar friends, and feels that at last the Carters are bettering themselves. As the champagne corks pop at midnight Susan would be in her seventh heaven…

But of course poor Susan hasn't got a chance. Neil's ideal way to see in the Millennium couldn't be more different. First of all he'd check that his pigs are all right, especially his favourite big sow. Then after he's had a pint (just the one) and Susan's had a sweet sherry in The Bull, they would climb together to the top of Lakey Hill and gaze at the stars in the sky, and the lights over towards Borchester.

What better place could Neil possibly be? Happy and contented, he'll head home for a nice hot cocoa before turning in. He'll tell the pigs in the morning that it is now the year 2000, not that they will care much. They'll be more interested in what's in his bucket.

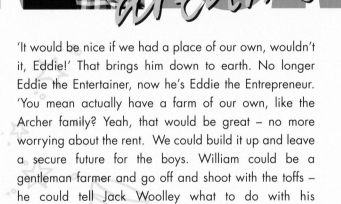

THE GRUNDYS OF GRANGE FARM

Life for Eddie and Clarrie Grundy has been a long succession of 'if onlys', so for them to be dreaming about what they might be doing at the New Year comes as no surprise. For all his bravado with the ladies, Eddie is really very fond of Clarrie and there's little doubt that he'd want them to celebrate together.

In Eddie's mind, the ideal place for him to start 2000 would be centre stage at the Grand Ol' Opry in Nashville, Tennessee. He'd stand there in the spotlight, strumming his guitar, while squealing girls from the Eddie Grundy fan club cluster in the wings, awaiting the moment when they can thrust themselves upon him. A constant shower of knickers would land at his feet from the adoring female multitude in the front rows, while somewhere in the wings an executive from a major record label is waiting to offer him a juicy contract… Sweet dreams!

Clarrie's fantasies are a little more practical. While Eddie's dreaming of Nashville, she'll whisper in his ear, 'It would be nice if we had a place of our own, wouldn't it, Eddie!' That brings him down to earth. No longer Eddie the Entertainer, now he's Eddie the Entrepreneur. 'You mean actually have a farm of our own, like the Archer family? Yeah, that would be great – no more worrying about the rent. We could build it up and leave a secure future for the boys. William could be a gentleman farmer and go off and shoot with the toffs – he could tell Jack Woolley what to do with his gamekeeper's job!'

'Then we could have a decent house,' says Clarrie, not missing a chance, 'with one of them futility rooms, so we don' t have to have all the washing hanging around.' She pauses for a moment. 'This is all very well Eddie, planning for the Millennium, but we're forgetting one thing. What would we do about Joe?'

Eddie is unperturbed, 'Oh, he'll be all right. There'll be plenty of room for him with the rest of the old folks in The Laurels!'

THE GREAT NEW GRUNDY GAME

Eddie Grundy is managed by Trevor Harrison

Hiya Fans! Here's a chance to have some fun of a cold winter's evening. Me and the boys dreamt this up one night when the telly was on the blink, and now they're playing it in The Bull. So here's your chance. Turn off the box and have a laugh. You know it's going to be simple because you know who invented it.

The aim of the game is to pick an Ambridge family and see if you know as much about them as you think you do. (I never play this with Mike Tucker because he's a mine of trivial information picked up on his milk round.) Any road, why not give it a whirl? Line up pints of Shires as prizes, and don't forget one for me when you're next in The Bull. Cheers!

You can play the game with two or more players, two or more teams.

HOME FARM

Q 1 What branch of the Services does Brian Aldridge come from?

Q 2 With whom did Brian have an affair in 1985?

Q 3 From which estate did Brian acquire Home Farm?

Q 4 What sort of swimming pool did the Aldridges have installed in 1978?

Q 5 Who is Debbie Aldridge's father?

Q 6 Which university did Debbie attend?

Q 7 Where did Debbie celebrate her 21st birthday?

Q 8 What unpleasant experience did Debbie and Kate have in the village in 1993?

Q 9 Who was the father of Jennifer's son Adam?

Q 10 Who was Jennifer Aldridge's father?

Q 11 What was the name of the Aldridges' au pair?

Q 12 Which ladies' college did Kate join in 1988?

Q 13 What sort of fish would you find in Brian's fishing lake?

Q 14 What is the name of Brian and Jennifer's youngest child?

Q 15 What accident befell Brian at Grange Farm?

Q 16 By what name did Kate first call her daughter in 1998?

Q 17 Which new animal did Brian start farming in 1987?

Q 18 What is the name of Brian's mother-in-law?

Q 19 What is the name of Jennifer's sister?

Q 20 With whom did Jennifer Aldridge write *Ambridge – an English Village Through The Ages*?

BRIDGE FARM

Q 1 Which Bridge Farm Archer was born with a dislocated hip?

Q 2 Where did Pat Archer come from?

Q 3 Pat Archer was appointed Captain of what?

Q 4 Pat irritated Tony when she changed their paper from the *Daily Express* to what?

Q 5 Who was Roger Coombes?

Q 6 Who are Tony Archer's sisters?

Q 7 What connection did Jim Eliott have with Bridge Farm?

Q 8 What type of farming method is practised at Bridge Farm?

Q 9 What relation was Mrs P to Tony?

Q 10 When Pat returned to Tony after a separation, which Greek island did he take her to?

Q 11 Who ran a mobile disco?

Q 12 What did John Archer always try to sell at Christmas?

Q 13 Who did John Archer try to impress by blowing £200 on a new suit?

Q14 To whom did the pony Comet belong?

Q 15 Tony ran over Marmaduke. Who or what was Marmaduke?

Q 16 What did John Archer do the night before he died?

Q 17 What was the name of the cottage that John and Hayley shared together?

Q 18 What did Hayley and Tommy keep on losing?

Q 19 Owing to a misunderstanding between Tommy and Hayley, what did Tom Forrest's prize marrow end up as?

Q 20 Where did Helen and her cousin Kate spend time smoking and drinking cider in their early teens?

First: Get some paper and pens
Second: Choose a family

    a) The Aldridges of Home Farm
    b) The Archers of Bridge Farm
    c) The Archers of Brookfield
    d) The Grundys of Grange Farm

Third: Stop arguing – someone's got to be the Aldridges.
Now this is what you do:

Ask a question about your opponent's family. Your opponents write down the answer. Take it in turns until you've asked each other ten questions. Swap papers and turn to page 96 for the answers. Whoever has the least points is the loser and pays for the Shires!

BROOKFIELD FARM

Q 1 On which estate were the Archers tenant farmers?

Q 2 In what year did Phil's wife Grace die in a fire?

Q 3 What relation was Tom Forrest to Phil?

Q 4 At Brookfield, who did Nigel Pargetter accidentally get into bed with?

Q 5 What did Phil replace in 1991?

Q 6 Who did Jill publicly humiliate by telling them exactly what she thought of them?

Q 7 What line of work did Kenton originally go into?

Q 8 On which railway station did Phil propose to Jill?

Q 9 Which of Phil and Jill's children was born with a hole in the heart?

Q 10 Where did Cameron Frazer abandon Elizabeth?

Q 11 Who jilted David Archer?

Q 12 Which county does Ruth Archer come from?

Q 13 Which Agricultural College did Ruth attend?

Q 14 What was the name of the Estate Agents where Shula used to work?

Q 15 Which Brookfield worker used to call Phil 'Master Phil'?

Q 16 Who is Phil Archer's sister?

Q 17 What 'diversification' did Jill begin in 1990?

Q 18 Who were Blossom and Boxer?

Q 19 Which was the first newspaper Elizabeth joined as a journalist?

Q 20 When Dan and Doris left Brookfield, where did they move to?

GRANGE FARM

Q 1 Who was Eddie engaged to before Clarrie?

Q 2 Who was Eddie's singing partner?

Q 3 Why did Eddie name one of his ferrets after Mrs Archer?

Q 4 Which Radio 1 DJ returned Eddie's cassettes?

Q 5 Eddie played the same part in two rival productions of the same pantomime on the same night. What was the panto?

Q 6 What is the name of Clarrie's sister?

Q 7 Why did Clarrie begin a new diet in 1981?

Q 8 Who was Clarrie's father?

Q 9 What was Joe's wife called?

Q 10 What illness does Joe suffer from (allegedly)?

Q 11 Who is William Grundy's godmother?

Q 12 What did William put in his mother's freezer?

Q 13 Where did Clarrie want Eddie to buy a farm?

Q 14 What is the name of Joe's eldest child?

Q 15 Edward Grundy Junior was not born in Ambridge. Where was he born?

Q 16 Who is Borsetshire's greatest Country & Western star?

Q 17 Which film star did the Grundys meet at the Birmingham Hippodrome?

Q 18 Which World Cup match did Joe and Eddie sell tickets for?

Q 19 Where did Eddie serenade Clarrie after a long coach journey?

Q 20 What was the name of the poor old Grundy dog who died because of the barn fire at Grange Farm?

Any dispute about the answers should be referred to Eddie Grundy and *not* to the *Archers Annual*

THE WOOLLEYS OF GREY GABLES

If only Jack had asked Peggy how she would like to see in the New Millennium. He hadn't, although she'd been dropping hints throughout the year. Had she been asked she would have said straight away that she had always wanted to go with Jack on a luxury cruise across the Atlantic. They'd have a state room and sit at the Captain's table every night. Then they would sail up the Hudson River past the statue of Liberty and right into the heart of New York City…

Perhaps they'd stay in a skyscraper hotel on 42nd Street, go to Macy's and Tiffany's, stroll across Central Park and down Fifth Avenue before having a luxurious dinner surrounded by attentive waiters. Then they'd ride the elevator to the top of the Empire State Building and watch the lights and fireworks over Manhattan as midnight struck.

Of course there was always the slight concern that they might just bump into Peggy's former G.I. boyfriend Conn. 'It's a lovely thought,' sighs Peggy, 'but it's hardly likely to happen.'

Although he wouldn't admit it to anyone (least of all to Peggy), Jack would like to see in the Millennium in Stirchley where he spent many a New Year's Eve as a boy. But he'd like it to be as it was, with back-to-back houses and the foundry at the end of the road. He'd share the celebrations with the folk he grew up with. 'I wonder where they all are now? We didn't have any money, but we certainly knew how to enjoy ourselves.'

THE TUCKERS OF WILLOW FARM

Mike Tucker will be facing up to the New Millennium with mixed feelings. Things haven't gone well for him and Betty over the past few years. Sometimes all that's kept them going is the belief that things can only get better.

How would Mike like to spend New Year's Eve? It may come as a surprise to know that he has a burning ambition to go on the stage. Not that he would agree to take part if Larry Lovell or Lynda Snell approached him, but ever since he went to see *A Midsummer Night's Dream,* Mike has thought to himself, 'I could do as good as that'.

Then it occurred to him that, having only one eye, he was a dead cert to play Long John Silver in *Treasure Island*. As he collected up the money on his milk round he could be heard muttering 'pieces of eight, pieces of eight'. And many's the time the milk float has turned into the drive of Willow Farm to the sound of 'Fifteen men on a dead man's chest'.

Betty doesn't know of this ambition, and if she did she'd probably tell Mike not to be so daft, and Roy would turn puce with embarrassment. Even so, if there is a company within reasonable distance of Ambridge that's doing *Treasure Island* this year, and they happen to be looking for a Long John Silver…

Betty's treasure island would be one where she could lie in the sun under a shady palm tree, and listen to the sea while a succession of bronzed young men carried out her every wish. 'Not much chance of that,' she's been heard to say. 'The shop's not been doing too well recently, and Mr Woolley is always anxious that takings should rise over Christmas, so he's unlikely to let me go. Still, a couple of days with my sister down in Worthing would be the next best thing.'

When it comes to the Millennium, after a day like any other, Mike will probably turn to Betty and say 'Why don't we go down to The Bull then?' All worries will disappear when Mike and Betty join the other villagers of Ambridge to down a glass or two and wish everyone present a Happy New Year!

fact file

NAME: BRIAN ALDRIDGE
BORN: 20 November 1943
ADDRESS: Home Farm, Ambridge
OCCUPATION: Land owner
Director of Borchester Land
FAMILY: Married to Jennifer
Two daughters, Kate and Alice,
one stepson Adam, one
stepdaughter, Debbie
HOBBIES: Fishing, shooting,
swimming, womanising, flying,
skiing, the novels of GA Henty
SINS: Caroline Bone, Betty Tucker,
Mandy Beesborough

HIGHS

1975 Buys Home Farm with 1,500 acres from the Bellamys. Makes his mark as the first person in Ambridge to own a solar-powered swimming pool.

1976 Marries divorcee Jennifer Travers-Macy at Borchester Register Office.

1985 Has affair with Caroline Bone. Buys a 75% share in a horse she rides – Hassett Hill Two Timer.

1995 Diversifies by building an artificial lake for fly fishing and an off-the-road horse riding course.

1996 Becomes director and 'man on the spot' for Borchester Land consortium.

LOWS

1977 Birth of a daughter, Katherine Victoria (Kate); but Brian wants a son and heir.

1988 Another daughter, Alice Margaret, born.

1989 Struck by a cow with BSE, suffers a cerebral abcess and a post-traumatic epileptic fit. Worse still: can no longer drink or drive.

1998 Kate has an illegitimate child – and, to make matters worse, Brian discovers that the Tuckers are the other grandparents.

1999 Opposition by planning authorities scuppers plans to exploit investment by Borchester Land consortium.

What Brian didn't know...
Kate had added cannabis to the casserole he so enjoyed at the holiday cottage!

Like the squires of old, Brian enjoys shooting and fishing, and pursues his *droit de seigneur* wherever he gets the chance, even with a surprised Betty Tucker. Sadly, he's failed to uphold the other great tradition of the landed gentry, generosity towards his tenants, as the Grundys discovered to their cost when they asked for more time to pay the rent. 'Sorry, I've done what I can,' responded Brian – but what he really meant was that charity begins at home. His standing among the villagers of Ambridge is not high and people are rightly suspicious of his various business ventures, knowing that he will always put his own interests first. The village has been especially concerned by Bealtech's trial plot of oilseed rape at Home Farm, genetically modified for herbicide resistance.

His farm, the largest in Ambridge, gives Brian the sizeable income he needs to maintain the luxurious lifestyle he and his family enjoy.

Brian is a highly successful businessman and although there have been occasions when ventures have failed, they have never significantly impacted on the Aldridge bank account. However, he has been disappointed in his attempts to exploit the Berrow Estate, which he bought with a consortium of business colleagues after the disappearance of Simon Pemberton. They have met so far with limited success.

Brian should have known the consortium would expect a quick return for their investment. But he could not have anticipated farm prices would fall with such a resounding bump or the resultant impact on Estate revenue. The consortium have put forward several money-making schemes – all so far rejected by the planning authority.

So now he's got to come up with more than bright ideas. He's facing the constant attacks of Matthew Crawford at the Borchester Land board meetings, and the painful indignity of having accountants forced on him to examine the books. Brian may be down, but he's not out: he's a wily operator, and will doubtless land on his feet.

Brian is more successful in business than in dealing with family relationships. He's used to being at odds with Kate, but it's elder stepdaughter Debbie who is currently giving him a headache. Her lover is old enough to be her father – so where does that leave Brian?

Charles Collingwood

Charles was born in New Brunswick, Canada, and was educated at Sherborne – also the alma mater of Brian Aldridge. He trained at RADA, worked in rep and exercised his talents as actor, presenter, commentator and voice-artist in children's TV. *Archers* fans will remember his performance in *The Archers Live* at the Watermill Theatre Newbury and Battersea Park.

Outside Ambridge, Charles featured on Noel Edmonds's *Telly Addicts* as the urbane Round Scorer, and tackled the role of God for the *Alexei Sayle Show*.

Charles enjoys cricket (he once played a fast bowler in *Inspector Morse*), golf and gardening. He is married to Judy Bennett, who plays Shula Hebden Lloyd.

Hatching the plot

Editor: **Vanessa Whitburn**
Agricultural Story Editor: **Graham Harvey**
The Writers: **Mary Cutler, Adrian Flynn, Simon Frith,
Caroline Harrington, Christopher Hawes, Peter Kerry,
Louise Page, Chris Thompson, Joanna Toye**
Senior Producer: **Keri Davies**
Producers: **Julie Beckett, Louise Gifford**
Archivist: **Camilla Fisher**

'How could Brian behave like that?'

'Shula doesn't know when she's well off'

'I just wanted to cry with joy for Lizzie'

'Poor Jill, I know how she feels'

These are just a few of the comments overheard from listeners to *The Archers*. You'd think they were talking about their own family or friends. There's a magic when a programme lures you into its trap so skilfully that you can find yourself debating what's going on in Ambridge as fiercely as if it were real.

There are some who think that the actors just make it up as they go along, which shows how cleverly the cast read their lines. Cows moo, tractors pass, birds sing and pints are pulled. It all happens so naturally. But in truth the stories which captivate our interest evolve over a long period of time, with contributions from all sorts of sources.

A month is a long time in Ambridge. Twenty-four episodes, four million listeners to satisfy and 52 characters to steer through a labyrinth of storylines. Join the editorial team, 15 dedicated professionals, at one of their monthly script meetings and find out what makes *The Archers* tick.

Cooped up in an office in Pebble Mill for the best part of a day, voices raised, scribbling furiously on notepads, gesticulating and laughing with the light of enthusiasm glinting in their eyes, these are the people who make it all happen, the creators of the world of Ambridge and the folk that inhabit it. What sounds so spontaneous on the radio emerges only after a long process of discussion and advice, of meticulous planning and hard, dedicated slog.

Editor Vanessa Whitburn chairs long-term script meetings two or three times a year, when she gathers together the nine writers, three producers, the agricultural editor and the archivist to look at where *The Archers* is going. Some storylines are planned two years in advance, perhaps more. This is where the team earmarks the major events to which the show has to respond – high on the list this year, of course, is the Millennium – and discusses the larger trends

WRITER'S BRIEF

General
The Archers tells the day-to-day story of a contemporary farming community. Fiction and fact are equally important and carefully balanced. In planning ahead, the team has to think of long-term dramatic development and yet be flexible enough to respond to current farming trends and issues.

Specific
You're joining the team at a time when the problems facing farmers are front-page international news. Inevitably this will influence storylines and must be reflected in the experiences of Ambridge's farming community. You also need to be sensitive to other real events: a drought, a fall in farm prices, the Millennium.

Plot
Every situation and storyline, whether large or small, short-term or long-term, must be developed and brought to a logical conclusion. Some ideas that seemed brilliant at the time might not seem so bright in the cold light of reason.

Characters
You need to know the characters through and through: what they wear, what they eat or drink, how they behave in an emergency or when they're in love. The characters themselves (like the actors who play them) are getting older and this will influence how they react to what's happening around them. Young Hayley walked out on John when he two-timed her with Sharon, but Jennifer Aldridge has turned a blind eye to Brian's indiscretions for years. Once you are truly familiar with the characters and their circumstances you can put your imagination to work on them.

and directions that mould the characters' lives. Then, with the long-term policy in place, it's the job of the monthly script meeting to hammer out the finer points of each batch of stories closer to the time of recording.

All the writers attend every meeting – it's a policy Vanessa introduced to foster continuity of plot and mood – but only four of them will be involved in actually writing that month's episodes. Each writer produces a week's worth of scripts – that's six shows, 24 for the month – and they must leave the monthly editorial meeting knowing exactly what's required of them. Once the meeting is over, specialist advice can be sought from *The Archers'* team of experts, who are always at the end of a phone to advise on matters

the anniversary of John's death, an event that coincides with John's younger brother Tommy's 18th birthday.

In preparation for today's meeting, writer Joanna Toye set down her thoughts on the emotional strain that Pat might be under, her sadness as the anniversary approached, and the ways in which that might be exploited dramatically. This sparks off a wealth of ideas among the editorial team. They decide that the trigger for Pat's eventual breakdown will be an innocent dose of flu. Pat is usually resilient but on this occasion she would find it difficult to get better, she would become uncharacteristically listless and depressed, and lose her usual grip on life.

Vanessa Whitburn   Chris Hawes   Adrian Flynn   Julie Beckett   Graham Harvey

of law, religion, medicine or farming. But the dramatic, human content of the show rests for the time being in the hands of the writers.

Not much, however, is left to chance. Let's take as an example one of 1999's major storylines, Pat Archer's nervous breakdown. The story started on air in February, reached a climax in April and continued through the summer – and it's the planning of these crucial episodes that are being discussed today, on a wintry afternoon in February. The initial idea for Pat's breakdown came over a year ago at one of the long-term script meetings, when the aftermath of John's death was under discussion. How would Pat cope with her son's loss? Vanessa felt that it wasn't in Pat's nature to deal with her grief straightaway; like many who have been bereaved, she wouldn't confront the loss until a long time after the event. So the team decided to time Pat's reaction around

Dozens of questions immediately arise. How will Tony deal with Pat's illness? Who will look after the dairy? What about the new doctor – what would he recommend? Who would help Pat to get over the trauma? Someone remembers Mike Tucker's nervous breakdown some years ago. He's not someone you'd imagine talking intimately with Pat, but that in itself would open up all sorts of possibilities in terms of character as well as drama.

The show's specialist advisers come into play. Producer Louise Gifford is armed with research on emotional breakdowns, and medical adviser John Wynn Jones has been consulted on the various forms Pat's illness might take, the available treatments and the likely time of recovery.

With the threads of the story and the professional advice which underpins its reality, the writers are now ready to hammer out a scene-by-scene synopsis of their week's episodes. Once everyone is in agreement, it's time for them to retreat to their computers and make the stories come alive through the mouths of the characters. On this occasion writer Adrian Flynn has to put Pat through the wringer: she can't stop crying, she finds it hard to breathe and starts hyperventilating. A terrified Tony calls the doctor…

Finally, everything comes back to Vanessa Whitburn and producer Julie Beckett. They edit the scripts, ask for rewrites, make sure that every week's episodes flow into the next, then hand over the finished result for typing and recording.

Now it's the turn of the actors who bring the words so skilfully to life that you'd never believe that it hadn't just happened right there in front of your very ears.

WHAT THE ADVISERS SAY

Roger Ede – Legal Matters
My main involvement arose out of a meeting with Vanessa Whitburn at the Law Society's conference in 1993. I took her to one side and said 'Given the seriousness of the case, we could send Susan Carter to prison.' She liked the idea straightaway.

Jeremy Martineau – Religion
The move to calling the vicar by his Christian name evoked quite a lot of angry responses from clergy wives back in the eighties. This seems rather humorous now, but at the time I think it revealed how slow the church was to adapt to the present age. I particularly enjoyed helping to create the character of the current vicar, Janet.

Mary Cutler

Joanna Toye

Peter Kerry

Any other business?

Graham Smith – Veterinary
My association with *The Archers* cropped up very suddenly. An out-of-the-blue phone call asking for clarification of a few technical points regarding Caroline's horse Ringo, turned into a few very long calls, followed by nearly 50 pages of script to look at in the middle of a very hectic run-up to Christmas.

Patrick Holden – Organic Farming
After appearing in BBC Radio 4's *On Your Farm* with Peter Segger, I suggested to Anthony Parkin, then agricultural story editor, that it might not be a bad idea to convert one of the Ambridge farms to organic production. We suggested Brookfield. The script meeting thought otherwise, and concluded that Pat and Tony's farm was the only realistic candidate. I'm a carrot-grower myself, so it's been interesting to guide Tony down the path along which I have already travelled.

Is there life after Ambridge?

Hundreds of actors have passed through Pebble Mill on their way to *Archers* immortality – some of them we loved, some of them we loved to hate. But what happens to the actors when they shake the dust of Ambridge from their feet? We caught up with a few of them...

WILLIAM GAMINARA
PLAYED: Dr Richard Locke
Left for Manchester
November 1998

We were sorry to see Doc Locke leave for Manchester after his tussle in the sheets with Shula.

But William's career as an actor and writer has gone from strength to strength in the last year. He played the deputy head of a comprehensive school in the BBC six-parter *Hope and Glory* starring Lenny Henry (shown in summer 1999). He has written for *The Lakes*, dramatised Rachel Morris's novel *Ella and the Mothers* for BBC television, and written a stage play set in a dubbing studio – 'a serious but funny drama featuring actors playing actors'. William is currently working on a six-part TV drama called *Smitten* for World Productions.

CELIA NELSON
PLAYED: Sharon Richards
Left Ambridge December 1997

Sharon was the siren who lured John Archer away from his beloved Hayley. After a long struggle, John tore himself away and returned to the arms of his true love, leaving Sharon out in the cold (and out of the show).

Celia retained an *Archers* connection, appearing in a production of Noël Coward's *Blithe Spirit* in Salisbury, directed by Gareth Armstrong – alias painter and decorator/Cat and Fiddle co-proprietor Sean Myerson.

SAM BARRISCALE
PLAYED: John Archer
Died in a tractor accident
February 1998

Although he was killed by an upturned tractor, John Archer is still mourned by the villagers of Ambridge – not least his mother Pat, whose delayed reaction to his death brought on a nervous breakdown.

Two years on Sam has several irons warming nicely in the fire. He's working on a television script of a father-and-son Irish drama, based on his own experiences, and has been seen in *Hetty Wainthropp Investigates* playing Dave Skerry, a shady smuggler of rare animals. Sam has also faced death in the electric chair in a gruesome silent short film made by a friend at the National Film School. They hope it will get a showing on Channel 4's *Shooting Gallery* showcase for new filmmakers.

RICHARD DERRINGTON
PLAYED: Mark Hebden
Killed in a car crash,
February 1994

Mark the sensible solicitor, Shula's first husband, was killed in a country lane, driving home from work, quite unaware that he was soon to become a father. Richard has recovered remarkably well from the accident, and appears regularly at Alan Ayckbourn's Scarborough Theatre, and this year has been on tour as a medium in Ayckbourn's *Haunting Julia*. He's also been seen on television in *Casualty, EastEnders* and *Heartbeat*.

DELAVAL ASTLEY
PLAYED: Cameron Fraser
Left Ambridge April 1992

Handsome rotter Cameron Fraser left pregnant Lizzie in a motorway café and drove out of *The Archers*, never to be seen around these parts again.

Since a 1998 Shakespeare tour through America, Delaval has taken to country life in a big way. He left the city with his wife and three children and moved into an early eighteenth-century farmhouse in north Norfolk, where he has been busy ever since on extensive renovations. Now, he says, there's only the decorating left to do. 'It was definitely the right move. We're all very happy.'

HUGH DICKSON
PLAYED: Guy Pemberton
Died of a heart attack, April 1996

Caroline still wishes her husband Guy had not departed this life quite so suddenly. *Archers* listeners heard his heart attack happen down a phone line, and feared the worst.

Hugh, on the other hand, is very much alive, and recently appeared opposite Joely Richardson in *The Echo* and as a judge in *Kavanagh QC*.

Further from home he has appeared at Al Bustan, Lebanon's Garden Festival held high up in the hills outside Beirut, where Hugh and Lebanese-born actress Valerie Sarruf put on a highly successful programme of verse and prose readings on the theme of Poland.

Hugh also tours round Britain with actress Anne Harvey in a recital programme on the poet Walter de la Mare, and was pleased to be joined on stage at the Cheltenham Festival by two of de la Mare's grandchildren.

TIM MEATS
PLAYED: Rev. Robin Stokes
Left Ambridge 1994

Robin was devastated when Caroline broke off their engagement, and decided to move out of the diocese right away. But he is still friendly with Alistair Lloyd and may one day make a surprise visit to Ambridge.

In the meantime Tim has been on a seven-month tour playing the Prince Escalus in *Romeo and Juliet*. He has also been in three productions at the Salisbury Playhouse: Noël Coward's *Hay Fever,* David Hare's *Racing Demon* and Chekhov's *The Cherry Orchard*.

On television he's appeared in *Body Guards* and *Silent Witness*, but hasn't done much radio (a shame with that lovely voice); his last appearance was in *Eric the Viking* three years ago.

fact file

NAME: TOM FORREST
BORN: 20 October 1910
DIED: 5 November 1998
LAST ADDRESS: The Laurels Nursing Home, Ambridge
OCCUPATION: Retired game-keeper
FAMILY: Married to Pru, fostered two sons Johnny Martin, Peter Stevens
HOBBIES: Growing prize vegetables, shooting, dominoes
PAST SINS: Shot and killed Bob Larkin

HIGHS

1958 Marries Pru Harris.

1960 Moves into Keeper's Cottage, built for him by Charles Grenville. Fosters Johnny Martin and his friend Peter Stevens.

1976 Retires as Jack Woolley's head keeper to run Woolley's new garden centre with Pru, and after that his fish farm.

1987 Delighted when Peter Stevens turns up unexpectedly at a surprise party given for Pru.

LOWS

1957 Accidentally shoots Bob Larkin, and is charged with manslaughter.

1958 Pru goes away to a sanatatorium for six months when a shadow shows up on her lung. Tom misses her desperately.

1991 After her second stroke, Pru goes to live in the Laurels nursing home; Tom is lost without her.

1998 Tom finally joins Pru at the Laurels but hates giving up his independence.

What if…

Tom hadn't shot Bob Larkin? Bob might have married Pru and Tom would have been left on his own.

When Tom Forrest died, Ambridge lost one of its oldest and best loved inhabitants, and one of its most distinctive voices. It's hard to believe that his country burr will never be heard again in shop, church or pub.

Tom was born and raised in the old traditions of Ambridge and English country life, with generations of reverence and service to the gentry behind him. It was natural that he should follow in his father's footsteps and become the Squire's game-keeper, quickly establishing himself as the best man for the job with his unequalled knowledge of the land and the birds that he bred for the shooting season.

Throughout his working life, Tom had a number of different employers – Squire Lawson-Hope, his son Charles Grenville, Ralph Bellamy and Jack Woolley – but he treated them all the same. If he thought the birds weren't ready or the shoot wasn't being conducted properly he told them so, and argue though they might he always got his way in the end.

Tom hated any predator that came too close to his beloved game, but it was for poachers that he reserved special odium. It was while stalking poachers that Tom accidentally shot and killed Bob Larkin and was charged with manslaughter. No one who knew Tom believed he was guilty and there was great rejoicing when he was acquitted.

It wasn't always easy for Tom to keep up with the pace of change in Ambridge. Brought up as a pillar of the C of E, he found it hard to accept the ordination of women and for a while stopped worshipping at St Stephen's when Janet Fisher became the new vicar.

Tom's garden at Keeper's Cottage was his pride and joy. His fruit and veg regularly carried off the prizes at the Flower and Produce Show, while Pru rejoiced in similar success with her cakes and jam. Trouble loomed when neighbour Hayley Jordan confessed to turning Tom's prize exhibition marrow into jam, mistaking it for a gift; happily for Hayley, he saw the funny side, especially when her attempt to repair the damage by entering his second-best specimen was crowned with success and a First Prize rosette.

Tom was a sociable soul, never happier than when smoking his pipe and playing dominoes in The Bull or chinwagging with 'that silly old fool' Walter Gabriel. He kept his singing voice to the end, and was frequently asked to perform his folk songs of a Friday night, often finishing with his favourite, The Village Pump.

Tom's death came unexpectedly. Unable to cope on his own any longer he joined Pru at The Laurels, a local nursing home, and died shortly afterwards. Within four days Pru was dead as well. They were given a joint funeral, their coffins taken to the church on a horse-drawn carriage.

Bob Arnold

Bob Arnold made the part of Tom so very much his own that it was hard to tell 't'other from which'. Both Bob and Tom were born in the country, both were singers of country folk songs, enjoyed a good pint of bitter and were respected by their colleagues.

Bob came into broadcasting by chance. Already renowned for his folksongs and stories of Cotswold life, he was an automatic choice for a new Home Service programme *In the Cotswolds* broadcast from Burford. Amazingly, when Bob auditioned for the new serial, *The Archers*, he was initially turned down because his accent was thought to be too recognisable. However, wisdom prevailed and finally he was cast as Doris Archer's brother, Tom Forrest.

For more than 30 years Bob set the tone for the Sunday omnibus edition, prefacing it with a nugget of topical country folklore before describing the week's events in Ambridge. When Bob died in 1998 it was fitting that the character he had played for so long should die too.

BRIDGE FARM

TYPE:
Organic dairy
ACREAGE:
172
PRINCIPAL PRODUCTS:
Organic milk for yoghurt
and ice cream
CURRENT STATE:
Buoyant
PROSPECTS FOR 2000:
Very good

When Tony and Pat Archer decided to 'go organic' at Bridge Farm, there were plenty of neighbours just waiting for the business to go belly up. But now, 15 years later, it's impossible to deny the wisdom of the decision. With growing concern about the safety of chemical contamination, organic food is reaching mainstream consumers as never before. It was Pat's idea to produce organic yoghurt and ice cream, sold in Underwoods, the Borchester department store, and through a specialist wholesaler.

It's not exactly a story of overnight success, though. Long before they could register as a fully organic farm, Tony and Pat had to stop using artificial fertilisers and pesticides and stop treating the dairy herd with antibiotics as a routine matter. Only after the agreed term of four years would the Soil Association check that the land was free of contamination and then finally reward them with official recognition as an organic farm.

Entrepreneurial Pat adds value to the premium organic milk by turning it into their yoghurt and ice cream. She runs the dairy with part-time help including Clarrie Grundy, Colin Kennedy and Brenda Tucker, while daughter Helen, full of ideas from agricultural college, does her best to inject new ideas into the business.

With its small fields, largely watered by streams, Bridge Farm is ideal for dairy farming. Tony and Tommy cope with a herd of 65 Friesian milkers and 40 other cattle, together with their acreage of barley, wheat, and a mixture of organic root vegetables. There is also a small area given over to the production of cabbages and leeks. Tony had hoped to follow local tradition and hand Bridge Farm over to his oldest son, but John was killed in a farming accident. Younger son Tommy took over his brother's pigs and built up a successful small business selling organic pork and sausages. Tony occasionally uses contract labour and equipment for the harvest and silage, and takes on students to help out at busy times.

Pat and Tony are very proud of their success at Bridge Farm and often give advice to other farmers thinking of turning organic, and farm walks and open days are an occasional feature at Bridge Farm.

GRANGE FARM

TYPE:
Tenant holding, mainly dairy
ACREAGE: 118
PRINCIPAL PRODUCTS:
Milk, turkeys for Christmas
CURRENT STATE:
Desperate to keep afloat

It's not much bigger than a small-holding. It looks dilapidated and run-down. The access is difficult and the land awkward to plough. Yet there is a family living in that ramshackle farmhouse. Their cows produce enough milk to warrant the tanker calling, they can some-times get credit from Borchester Mills, and they only just manage to pay their twice-yearly rent.

Grange Farm is part of the Berrow Estate, owned by Borchester Land. Joe Grundy is the tenant, living at the farm with his son Eddie, daughter-in-law Clarrie, and grandsons William and Edward. The truth is that with 120 acres it's too small to run profitably under present-day methods. Time and again the Grundys have faced disaster, only to be rescued at the last minute.

They thought it was the end in 1996 when the farm caught fire destroying the milking parlour and their Friesian herd.

But they managed to get compensation and re-stocked with a fine herd of Jersey cows.

A Notice to Remedy has been served on Grange Farm on more than one occasion, due to the state of general disrepair of the farm – but Joe is always quick to point out that the farm buildings are the responsibility of the landlord.

It seems that every change in farming practice, be it milk quotas, EU regulations or Health and Safety rules, brings Grange Farm

and the Grundys another step down the slippery slope. The monthly milk cheque is their lifeline, and there's always the hope that their number will come up on the National Lottery! Both Joe and Eddie try various money-making schemes with little success, while it's up to resilient Clarrie to work two jobs in order to keep the family clothed and

fed. To give Eddie his due he's always willing to turn his hand to hedging or delivering farm manure if it will help towards the rent, but there are too many small contractors like him chasing a severely limited amount of work.

It's a wise young William Grundy who has no wish to inherit the tenancy of Grange Farm, seeing his future as a gamekeeper at Grey Gables.

The Grundys have been a thorn in the flesh in Ambridge for decades. Simon Pemberton tried to evict them, and Borchester Land would turn Grange Farm over to housing if they could. But whatever happens, the Grundys are well used to picking themselves up, shaking themselves down, and starting all over again!

BROOKFIELD FARM

TYPE:
Mixed
ACREAGE:
469
PRINCIPAL PRODUCTS:
Milk, pigs, sheep,
cereals
**Current state: Stable,
but affected by world
markets**

The key to Brookfield's success is its variety. As a mixed farm, not specialising in any particular branch, it is well placed to cope with the unpredictable nature of the British farming business.

There is a large herd of milk-producing Friesians, which narrowly escaped TB earlier this year, more than 100 other cattle, 60 sows to provide baconers, a flock of 300 ewes and a small number of free-range hens providing eggs for the farmhouse and family. The grassland at Brookfield now extends over 258 acres, having absorbed parts of adjoining farms at intervals over the years. Cereals and oil-seed rape are grown in rotation with other crops, while eight acres have been designated as set-aside. Ten acres of beet are grown for fodder, 12 acres are down to beans, while potatoes are planted on 15 acres.

For more than 30 years Phil has been the mainstay of Brookfield Farm, ready to cope with any problem or take over a job as required. Once he was assisted by a faithful band of employed farm hands; now Ruth and David do most of the work, with Bert Fry their only regular employee. They also use occasional contractors and casual labour for silage, sheep-shearing, harvest and so on. Brookfield also has a contract from Borchester Land to farm 570 arable acres.

This year, Brookfield is undergoing the biggest change in its recent history as Phil starts to hand over the reins to David and Ruth. Phil has accepted that the younger generation are ready for greater responsibility, but David's unlikely to get things all his own way: his dad still takes a passionate interest in the land that means so much to him

Jill is looking forward to Phil accepting retirement at last. Maybe she'll be able to tempt him off the farm for an occasional holiday. He'll certainly have more time to chat to his favourite Middle White sow, Molly.

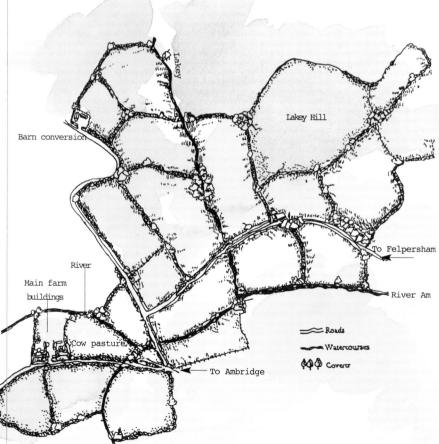

HOME FARM

TYPE:
Mainly arable
ACREAGE:
1655
PRINCIPAL PRODUCT:
Quality grain, sheep, deer
CURRENT STATE:
Biggest farm in Ambridge
PROSPECTS FOR 2000:
Appear to be sound

While Brookfield Farm provides a picture of a traditional family farm, Home Farm is most definitely a product of the twentieth century.

It was originally created out of the amalgamation of several holdings. Additional purchases over the years have turned it into the biggest farm in the area, currently standing at 1,655 acres. The fields are large, mostly over 60 acres; the largest, over 100 acres in size, has grown at the expense of ancient hedgerows, much to the anger of local conservationists.

The owner of Home Farm, Brian Aldridge, recognises that he has a responsibility to care for the countryside. But, as a business-man, his prime objective in farming is to maximise his profit.

Diversification is one way to do that, and canny Brian has even put the set-aside land to good use: there's a 25-acre horse riding course, an artificial lake for fly fishing, a deer compound with 110 hinds, stags and calves, and facilities for shooting game. Since Brian was able to combine his shooting with the Berrow Estate's, he employed a full-time gamekeeper, and has taken over Grey Gables shoot too.

The lifestyle of the Aldridges can be measured by the type of vehicles in the garage, and the size of the swimming pool. Home Farm is the only Ambridge farm to have such a luxury.

It's not all fun and games down on Home Farm: alongside the leisure activities there is a good deal of more traditional farming going on. As well as the deer, the main stock is 600 ewes. Although Brian brings in contractors from time to time, the farm is well mechanised with a huge combine harvester, six tractors and a selection of regularly maintained farm machinery. Of the land itself more than 800 acres are put down to cereals, 270 acres are kept as grassland, and there's a small acreage of oil-seed rape and 100 acres of sugar beet.

There are still 80 acres of woodland at Home Farm, and in a rare moment of generosity Brian has donated a small area for the creation of a Millennium Wood with saplings and bluebells planted by the villagers. Brian's wife, Jennifer, has insisted that it should be named the Aldridge Millennium Wood. Some villagers, thinking perhaps that in a hundred years time no-one will remember Brian Aldridge, prefer to call it the Ambridge Millennium Wood.

fact file

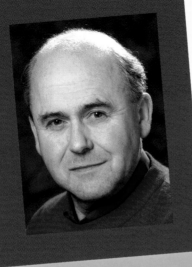

NAME: NEIL CARTER
BORN: 22 May 1957, Oxfordshire
ADDRESS: 1 The Green, Ambridge
OCCUPATION: Pig man. Farm worker
One-time feed rep for
Borchester Mills
FAMILY: Married to Susan
(née Horrobin). One daughter,
Emma, one son, Christopher
HOBBIES: Cricket, football,
bell-ringing
SINS: Convicted of possessing
drugs (wrongly).
Maureen Travis (nearly)

HIGHS

1977 Dates Ellen Padbury, the voluptuous Miss Ambridge 1977, much to the envy of the entire male population of Borsetshire.

1983 Bill Insley suggests they set up a farm-sharing scheme at Willow Farm.
Dirty weekend with the lovely Susan Horrobin.

1984 Susan walks down the aisle, radiant in white with her bump hardly showing at all.

1984 Bill bequeathes him eight acres and a barn for his hens.

1993 Maureen Travis offers chocolate biscuits and much, much more, but Neil stays faithful to Susan.

1999 Back to the land with regular work at Bridge Farm.

LOWS

1973 Sandy Miller passes him a joint at a party. Unlucky Neil is charged with possession of drugs, found guilty, put on probation and sentenced to community service.

1988 Son Christopher John born with cleft palette and harelip.

1999 Endures Susan's cries of 'not enough money – we need a bigger house'.

What if...
Shula had responded to the torch Neil carried for her?

Neil has found it difficult to make ends meet since losing his job as a sales rep for Borchester Mills. He's been getting by with a bit of general agricultural work – a spot of ploughing here, a little hedging there, growing strawberries and chopping logs. When he was obliged to accept Marjorie Antrobus's kind offer of a job digging her garden, he thought he'd hit rock bottom – but Neil, being a philosophical soul, simply gritted his teeth, took solace in his pigs and waited for something better to come along. Which it did: now he's getting regular work at Bridge Farm, but what he needs is a proper job.

Neil has come a long way since he arrived at Brookfield, a young apprentice who caused nothing but trouble until he started to learn a few basic principles of farming. Phil Archer was the first to recognise his passion for pigs and put Neil in charge of the Hollowtree pig unit. Later he set up on his own. Fancy-free Neil sowed his wild oats, and broke a few hearts including his own before putting Susan Horrobin in the club and dutifully marrying her.

All was going well at this stage: Neil's business had grown from small beginnings with a few hens to full-scale pig rearing when Bill Insley left him a barn and eight acres of land at Willow Farm. But Susan, having broken free from her Horrobin roots, wasn't content with life as a mere pigman's wife, and wanted a husband with regular hours and a regular income. When Borchester Mills advertised for a feed salesman, Susan persuaded Neil to buy a suit and apply for the job – which he got.

Reluctantly Neil handed in his notice to Phil and took to the road with his order book, insisting only on one thing – that he should still be allowed to keep his own pigs. Susan was happy, but not for long; implicated in her brother Clive's jailbreak, she ended up with her own six-month prison sentence after being found guilty of perverting the course of justice. Neil stood by her, looked after the children, his job and, of course, his pigs. Then one day, temptation arrived in the form of lonely farmer's wife Maureen Travis who offered Neil tea, sympathy, and rather more… Neil resisted, faithful to his marriage vows despite the fact that his wife was languishing in prison.

After Susan's release the couple struggled to get back on an even keel. Neil left his job when Borchester Mills treated the Grundys badly, after Neil had given them his word about paying off a debt in stages. He wasn't sorry to leave – nine-to-five had never suited him. Now, however, remained the much grimmer prospect of trying to break the news to Susan. She wasn't happy, but at least Neil is. He's back on the land, and that, after all, is his first love.

Brian Hewlett

Who would have thought that an actor who once played one of Tom Forrest's adopted sons, Johnny, would emerge some years later as the hard-working Neil? Such are the diverse talents of Brian Hewlett, who has played Neil since 1973.

Brian began his career in 1959 at Bernard Miles's Mermaid Theatre in London, when it opened to acclaim with productions of *Lock Up Your Daughters*, *Great Expectations* and the Christmas favourite *Treasure Island*. Decades of stage work followed (Brian makes an unforgettable panto dame), as well as a spell with the BBC Radio Drama Company and numerous TV roles.

Brian lives in Norfolk where he enjoys watching and photographing nature, a hobby that's taken him as far afield as Peru, Kenya and Rwanda, where he was able to observe rare mountain gorillas. It's a long way from Neil's pigs.

A MAGNIFICENT OBSESSION

Who is The Archers' number one fan?
Peter Tewkesbury has a good claim to the title –
as anyone who steps inside his house will
soon discover

Peter Tewkesbury is an avid collector of *Archers* memorabilia. His house in Horsham, Sussex, is full from floor to ceiling with every conceivable kind of *Archers* souvenir. There are more than 100,000 items, ranging from early scripts and picture mementos to films, tapes and videos, including the original copy of the *Archers'* signature tune 'Barwick Green' on a green label 78rpm record issued by Boosey and Hawkes. It's become a lifetime habit, and he's adding to the collection all the time.

Peter also has an encyclopaedic knowledge of everything to do with *The Archers* from the word go. For example, do you know the name of the actress who played Doris Archer in the original episodes?

Join us on a guided tour of Peter's extraordinary collection...

I was nine years old when the first national edition of *The Archers* was broadcast on the Light Programme on 1 January 1951. I listened to it with great interest because we were living in Cornwall at the time, and I was born in Birmingham and I knew that the programme came from the BBC studios at 282 Broad Street.

That gave me my first connection, and I suppose you could say I've been hooked on it ever since. Mind you, I've always been a great radio fan and loved listening to *Children's Hour*. I'm a radio man through and through. I've no time for television soaps like *EastEnders* or *Coronation Street*.

I haven't missed an episode of *The Archers* for the past ten years, and try to catch all the repeats and the omnibus edition as well. You can go to Ambridge every day in your mind. You can see these people and they become part of your family. I like to meet the faces behind the voices, which of course I can do now, at the Archers Addicts Conventions and other events. I remember walking round the 1992 Country Living Fair in London with Christine Barford (Lesley Saweard) and pinching myself, thinking, 'I can't believe it. Here I am walking round with Christine Barford!'

I haven't yet met Margot Boyd, who plays Marjorie Antrobus, or Julia Pargetter, played by Mary Wimbush, although I have heard them both in countless Radio 4 plays, as well as in *The Archers*. I've still to meet Tim and Siobhan Hathaway – the doctor and his wife – but it's early days yet and I expect I'll catch up with them soon.

Looking back over the years, I think the best love story there has ever been was the relationship between John Tregorran and Carol Grey. They seemed to be made for one another, and they had a lengthy courtship, which at the time didn't come to anything. Both married other people, but eventually they got together. I found it all very romantic. In fact, I wake up every morning looking at the cheerful

face of Carol Grey (Anne Cullen) in a cast group shot from the 1950s on the wall of our bedroom. It's such a happy picture; it just starts the day right.

Basil Jones, the original John Tregorran, died last year. I am trying to arrange a Memorial Day for him as he played such an important role in my favourite storyline.

I started collecting *Archers* memorabilia in 1971, when I bought a copy of the first edition of the *Borchester Echo* which was published in 1958, and it has just gone on from there. I keep my eyes open for pieces to add, and you find them in the most unlikely places, sometimes even at Steam Fairs. Now the word has got around about my collection people are very kind and send me things.

Space is becoming a problem as the collection grows. At the moment it's all carefully housed in cupboards; I can only lay it all out on special occasions like this, or it would take over every room in the house.

Luckily I was left a small nest-egg which enabled me to buy Tony Shryane's collection when it came up at auction. Tony was the programme's first producer and his collection included the first script, photographs and scrapbooks lovingly compiled by cast members. It spanned 28 years of *The Archers* and I got it for a hefty £850, but I couldn't let it go to anyone else.

I bought the 78rpm studio record of 'Barwick Green' from Deirdre Adams, née Alexandra, who was *The Archers'* secretary for the first 15 weeks of production. Once the record had been played 20 times it was discarded and replaced by a new copy. The old disc was given to Deirdre, and she had kept it all this time.

Apparently, when looking for a suitable signature tune, *Archers* creator Godfrey Baseley chose six 78s from the BBC record library, took them home and played them all. He singled out 'Barwick Green' as the best, and played it over and over again to see if he'd get tired of it before taking it back to the Broad Street studios. That version was used for several years before being replaced by a special BBC recording made by the BBC Midland Light Orchestra, before that too was superseded by the current stereo version.

I think my most treasured possession is a paperweight that was made to mark the 10,000th edition of *The Archers* in 1989. I value it because it actually belonged to Tony Shryane. He used it on his desk, and this makes it rather special for me. I've also got a flower-embroidered script and cast-list holder, which belonged to Pamela Mant who first played Christine Archer.

I've managed to collect almost all the promotional editions of the *Borchester Echo*. These were produced for publicity purposes over the years – in 1958, 1959, 1966 (featuring Sid Perks's wedding to Polly Mead), 1967, 1968, 1973, 1975 – celebrating 25 years since the regional edition of *The Archers*; 1981 to celebrate 30 years; and 1988. There was one published in 1961 to mark ten years of *The Archers*, which, as far as I can tell, is the only one missing from my collection. But you never know… (Hedli Niklaus subsequently discovered a copy of this missing link and donated it to Peter.)

In December 1996 Archers Addicts started publishing quarterly editions of the *Borchester Echo*, which of course I now receive through the post as part of my subscription package.

You may wonder at this train driver's hat I'm wearing. Well, my other great interest is steam trains, and I thought, 'Well, Eddie Grundy has a hat, so I must have a hat too.' To make it unique I've had Hollerton Junction added to the cap badge.

The other hat in my collection is William Grundy's hat (with a mini version of Eddie's famous horns), which I bought at an auction at Pebble Mill in 1994. Terry Molloy, who plays Mike Tucker, was the auction master who sold it to me.

One of the more unusual items in my collection is this egg box. I was out in the country one day, a typical Ambridge kind of area somewhere in Worcestershire or Warwickshire, when I spotted a house called Blossom Hill Cottage, with an 'eggs for sale' notice. I knocked on the door and said to the lady who answered: 'Do you realise this is Blossom Hill Cottage? Could I have half a dozen eggs, please?' She said: 'Yes, I know, and yes, you may', and produced the eggs in a box marked Brookfield Farm Eggs. I thought that was wonderful.

I am the proud possessor of two of the original Ambridge Originals! These organic pork sausages, well charred, were the very ones cooked

at the 1998 Royal Show at Stoneleigh, where *The Archers* recorded one whole episode. After Tommy and Hayley (Tom Graham and Lucy Davis) had recorded their scene, they handed out samples of their sausages to the public. The stall-holder who had cooked the batch had three left over and gave them to me. They've been in my freezer ever since.

The first ever mention of the programme in *Radio Times* was when it was known as *The Archers of Wimberton Farm*. The first of these five trial episodes went out on 29 May 1950 on the Midland Home Service and was such a success the BBC decided to run it nationally on the Light Programme in the New Year.

I am looking for more of the Lamplight series of Ambridge buildings in miniature. To be exact,

I still need The Bull, Brookfield, Blossom Hill Cottage and the shops. I only have two — Honeysuckle Cottage and Manor Court. Fellow Archers enthusiasts at my exhibitions seem to enjoy these miniatures, so I'd like to add to them.

There have been 50 books published relating to *The Archers*, and I have them all, and signed by the cast. The first book connected with *The Archers* was published in 1954 and is a sort of Who's Who of the 1950s. Another keen collector, Jan Stretch of Worcester, actually bought three copies of this book, and sold one on to me. We help each other out.

I am on the lookout for a plate which was made in 1985 showing the same picture as a pink, circular jigsaw that I have in my collection. If anyone has one of these that they can bear to part with I would be very happy to hear from them.

I travel to different parts of the country exhibiting my memorabilia collection, meeting other fans and collectors and raising

money for the Dyslexia Institute at the same time. It's like a travelling fair. I don't take any scripts or paper items on tour any more, as they are delicate and tend to get damp at fairs. At the moment I'm busy planning a special memorial exhibition at Godfrey Baseley's old school to celebrate *The Archers* 50th anniversary.

You want to know what my greatest ambition is? Well, it's one that I suppose will never happen in a month of Sundays, but I would dearly love to appear in an episode of *The Archers*. I don't want a starring role or anything; I'd be perfectly content to be one of the old boys propping up the bar at the Bull. One line would be enough. I'd just like to say, 'Another pint of Shires please, Sid'.

Hold the front page: *The Archers* has appeared on the cover of *Radio Times* regularly since the first year

Could it be Love?

*N*othing gets Archers audiences going like a bit of romance. Let's take a look at some of the passions simmering beneath the surface of Ambridge life and find out – will they or won't they? Did they or didn't they? Should they or shouldn't they?

Guy and Marjorie

The old are not immune to love and romance. Widow Marjorie Antrobus was delighted when gentlemanly landowner Guy Pemberton moved to Ambridge. A warm friendship grew up between them, which Marjorie would have liked to develop into something more than just sherry and bridge. Alas, Guy was more entranced by the attractive Caroline Bone, and Marjorie had to hide her feelings.

Marjorie had been lonely ever since her husband Teddy passed away. When she first moved to Ambridge she took a shine to Colonel Danby and offered to share her home with him – an invitation he gently declined.

After that she found herself answering a lonely hearts advertisement in the *Borchester Echo* ('gentleman farmer seeks companionship'); she was not pleased when none other than Joe Grundy turned up! Once she got over the shock she was sympathetic and helped him write to another applicant, and though they did have dinner together it went no further than that.

Kathy and Dave

Kathy is no angel. It wasn't so very long ago that Sid found out about her torrid affair with Detective Sergeant Dave Barry – and he was not pleased. Kathy had been very discreet and Sid only realised what had been going on a year after the affair ended. Dave foolishly sent Kathy a bottle of perfume and a Valentine card in a package with a St Albans postmark; Sid put two and two together, and took it so badly that he threw Kathy out of The Bull and actually started divorce proceedings. It took many months for that little episode to blow over.

Nigel and Caroline

People are often drawn together in times of trouble. Nigel Pargetter grew very close to Caroline Pemberton when he helped her get over the sudden death of her husband Guy. There were some particularly poignant moments when Nigel drove her to Suffolk to visit Guy's grave, by a willow tree at St Michael and All Angels church. This was definitely a 'will-they won't-they' situation; in the event both of them thought of Lizzie and managed to pull back from the brink.

Peggy and Conn

Who would have thought that a granddaughter would be instrumental in getting her grandmother to meet up with her wartime sweetheart? Kate Aldridge wrote the letter which reunited Peggy Woolley with former GI Conn Kortchmar. They talked late into the night about the good old days, how they'd won a Chinese fan for their jitterbugging and much more… so late that Conn had to spend the night at The Lodge wearing pyjamas lent by Peggy's disgruntled husband Jack.

Conn took Peggy on a nostalgic tour of his old wartime haunts, and wanted her to return with him to Boston. But Peggy found him too over-powering, and when a bouquet of flowers arrived Jack sent Conn packing. Ironically, the flowers had been sent by Kate as an apology for the trouble she had caused. Conn went away, leaving Peggy his Zippo lighter, a warming end to a fine romance.

Pat and Roger

Pat Archer fell in with Roger Coombes, her lecturer at Borchester Technical College when she was on a course in Women's Studies. Her marriage to Tony was going through a bad patch; Roger, who was waiting for his divorce to come through, had two children. They found they shared the same hopes and beliefs and grew very close. Gossip spread once they had been seen at The Feathers together. It was left to the vicar, Richard Adamson, to have a quiet word with Pat, who as a result, reluctantly brought the affair to an end.

Neil and Maureen

While Susan Carter was serving a prison sentence for assisting her brother Clive's escape from custody, Neil Carter fell into the arms of the needy Maureen Travis. It was Maureen ('call me Mo') who smoothed Neil's brow and made him cups of tea when he was disillusioned with his job as a salesman for Borchester Mills and running the family single-handed.

Neil very nearly succumbed. Once Susan was back home again Mo did her best to imply that it was much more than tea and sympathy. In the end, Neil had to come clean with Susan over the whole matter.

Clarrie, Austin and Roch

You wouldn't think that Clarrie Grundy had time for passion, but she has – particularly on holidays. There was, for instance, Austin the coach driver on the trip to Jersey, who was so smitten by Clarrie's charms that he wooed her with Christmas and Valentine cards. Eddie, consumed with jealousy, had himself tattooed.

Another journey, another man: Clarrie returned from the Meyruelle twinning trip obsessed by French-Canadian pop singer Roch Voisine, listened constantly to his songs and turned to Jean-Paul, the chef at Grey Gables, for translations of the lyrics. Eddie, getting the wrong end of the stick, found the words written out in Jean-Paul's handwriting and tried to punch the hapless chef, only succeeding in hurting his hand on the wall behind. Unabashed, Clarrie extended her new-found Francophilia into the kitchen and enlisted Jean-Paul's help with herbs and garlic for the dishes she now wanted to concoct.

Sid and Betty

Sid has always had a soft spot for Betty Tucker – an unspoken attraction that she fully reciprocates. Push nearly came to shove when Betty was having problems with Mike: he'd lost the sight of one eye in an accident, and took his depression out on Betty and the kids. Things got so bad that Betty took the children and moved into The Bull, where Sid was ready to offer much more than just a shoulder to cry on. Betty, unlike Jolene, did not give in to temptation.

Elizabeth and Hugh

Lizzie swore that her frequent meetings with Hugh were strictly business, but as we all know that's the oldest story in the book, and of course nobody believed her. She was away from home a good deal, while he was putting a good deal of business her way – and poor Nigel was being driven to distraction back at home. Finally, however, when Lizzie realised just how upset Nigel had become, she did the right thing and gave up her lucrative association with Hugh, returning instead to life and work at Lower Loxley.

All Addicts *together*

Addicted to The Archers? You don't have to be alone: you could join the 20,000 members of Archers Addicts. Prime mover Hedli Niklaus (left), alias The Bull's Kathy Perks, is your guide to four pages of fun, sun and fan worship.

The programme was approaching its 40th birthday, and the cast thought the best way of celebrating this momentous occasion was to create a fan club for the thousands of loyal listeners who had sustained us through the years. We had no idea it would be so successful, or that we would end up organising so many events. It's virtually taken over my life!

Many of us work in theatre and television, but nothing excites people like discovering that we're in *The Archers*. It's a great icebreaker. Even my niece's boyfriend is a fan – much to her disgust! Over 20,000 people have joined since we started, and the real hardcore fans know more about Ambridge than we do. They run *Archers* discussion days and arrange gatherings for charity. Many of them write to tell us how much they love the programme and what it means to them. Some of the letters are very touching; a six-page letter from a woman who had tried the same *in vitro* fertilisation programme as Shula but failed to get pregnant, another saying that *The Archers* is an extended family.

I like the fact that our fans come from all walks of life, truck drivers, lords and ladies, doctors and window cleaners. They have two things in common: a love of *The Archers* and a sharp sense of humour.

At one of our conventions a hard-bitten journalist gazed in awe at the chattering throng of people busy meeting the cast and enjoying themselves. 'This is weird,' he said, 'it's like a family wedding.' I knew exactly what he meant.

Some people don't want to meet the cast in case it shatters their illusions. But for most members, meeting the people behind the voices is the most exciting treat Archers Addicts offers.One of our most faithful fans, Vicky Griffiths, put it very well. 'Radio drama,' she says 'is all about the imagination, and I can easily make my own pictures again when I next listen.'

Above: *The discerning addict: Simon Dodds enjoys a good read*

Left: *Off to a great start: 40th Anniversary Tour. Pat Archer (Patricia Gallimore), Kenton Archer (Graeme Kirk), Mark Hebden (Richard Derrington) and Jack Woolley (Arnold Peters)*

Below: *Addiction starts young: Jill Archer (Patricia Greene) is impressed*

Win a trip to Ambridge! see page 69 for details

Above: *Monologue from George Barford*

Our sixth convention, the fourth to be held at Pebble Mill, and what a riot! Mike Tucker compered the show to raise money for St Stephen's bells. Lynda Snell's version of *Blind Date* was unforgettable, as was the sight of Susan and Neil Carter cavorting to 'I've Got You Babe'. Meanwhile the Grundys (sans Clarrie, of course) set up an Alternative Talent Contest in the BBC Club, which served as the Cat and Fiddle for the day. People didn't know what hit them! The highlight of the evening was the auction, with half the proceeds going to the RSPB. Jill's teapot fetched a fortune – as you'd expect…

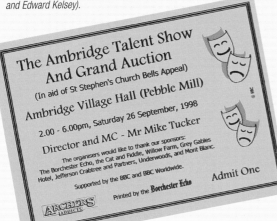

Above: *Welcome Party for the Lord Mayor of Birmingham. Left to right: William Grundy (Philip Molloy), Cllr Susan Anderson, editor Vanessa Whitburn, Eddie and Joe Grundy (Trevor Harrison and Edward Kelsey).*

Above: *Joe snatches a kiss from Lynda (Carole Boyd).*

Below: *Blind Date: Lynda Snell outdoes Cilla.*

The Ambridge Talent Show
And Grand Auction
(In aid of St Stephen's Church Bells Appeal)
Ambridge Village Hall (Pebble Mill)
2.00 - 6.00pm, Saturday 26 September, 1998
Director and MC – Mr Mike Tucker
The organisers would like to thank our sponsors:
The Borchester Echo, the Cat and Fiddle, Willow Farm, Grey Gables Hotel, Jefferson Crabtree and Partners, Underwoods, and Mont Blanc.
Supported by the BBC and BBC Worldwide.
Printed by the *Borchester Echo*
Admit One
ARCHERS ADDICTS

ARCHERS AWEIGH!
NOVEMBER 1998

Cruise to the Lands of the Crusades aboard P&O's *Victoria.* Sensational! Venice, Jerusalem, Cairo and Athens. Passengers included Jill Archer, Christine Barford, Joe and Eddie Grundy, Sean Myerson, Elizabeth Pargetter, Kathy Perks. A marvellous time was had by all and no-one got swept overboard. Baltic Capitals next!

Above: *The cast arrive in Venice. Front row, left to right: Sean Myerson (Gareth Armstrong), Elizabeth Pargetter (Alison Dowling), Christine Barford (Lesley Saweard), Eddie Grundy (Trevor Harrison). Back row, left to right: Joe Grundy (Edward Kelsey), editor Vanessa Whitburn, Jill Archer (Patricia Greene)*

AS GOOD AS GREY GABLES
MAY 1999

We've run several weekends at Wood Norton Hall, nestling in the heart of the Cotswolds, and we take the guests to locations which have been used for publicity and location recordings over the years, winding up at The Bull of course. We don't cook the delicious food but we act as hosts, and we pick an *Archers* actor with the gift of the gab to speak on the Saturday night. Very much black tie. We do our best to keep Eddie Grundy at bay but he has a habit of popping in unexpectedly.

Below: *Grey Gables (alias Wood Norton Hall)*

THE ARCHERS EXPERIENCE AT
BARTON HALL JUNE 1999

I suppose this is our version of a *Doctor Who* convention! Barton Hall is in Torquay. It's a crazy mock-gothic Victorian spread of a place owned by Pontins and overlooking Torbay. We assembled everyone we could think of — editor Vanessa Whitburn, senior producer Keri Davies, and loads of the cast. We ran workshops for would-be script-writers, gave a glimpse of how the programme is put together with sound engineer Louise Willcox, and ran bottle-top bingo with Mike Tucker (Terry Molloy). There was something for everyone with a Grey Gables Buffet, Eddie Grundy's disco and a one-off cabaret performance showing the cast's other talents — something completely different. May it be the first of many.

Left: *Eddie Grundy (Trevor Harrison) and Kathy Perks (Hedli Niklaus) host the quiz*

Above: *Susan Carter (Charlotte Martin) with friends*

FULL STEAM AHEAD ON THE ORIENT EXPRESS July 1999

Very distinguished this; very Lower Loxley! Evesham may not be Venice but passengers aboard the Orient Express, sipping champagne, were not complaining. An elegant setting for meeting members of the cast and taking home memories of a very special event.

ARCHERS ADDICTS COMPETITION: WIN AN EXCLUSIVE VISIT TO AMBRIDGE

Six lucky winners will go on a special guided tour to the heart of Ambridge – alias the BBC's Pebble Mill studios in Birmingham. You will meet and talk to the stars and listen in as they record the show – having first signed a vow of secrecy of course! Just answer the questions below, then tell us in no more than 50 words what you like best about *The Archers*.

1   Name four *Archers* characters who play musical instruments

2   Name all the inhabitants of:
    a   **Honeysuckle Cottage**
    b   **Nightingale Farm**
    c   **Lower Loxley Hall**
    d   **The Cat and Fiddle**

Post your entries to Archers Addicts, PO Box 1951, Moseley, Birmingham B13 9DD. Closing date 31 May 2000. The winners will be picked out of Eddie Grundy's hat. The best answers to the tie-breaker will be printed in the June issue of the *Ambridge Village Voice*, and there's an Archers Addicts mug for each one published.

Archers Addicts
PO Box 1951
Moseley
Birmingham
B13 9DD

telephone 0121 683 1951
fax 0121 683 1955
e-mail dum.di.dum@archers-addicts.com
website http://www.archers-addicts.com/

An English Country Gardener

Stefan Buczacki has probably talked to more British gardeners, presented more TV and radio programmes and written more about the subject than anyone else. He's also an avid Archers fan – so who better to delve into the beds and borders of Ambridge and solve some of the villagers' horticultural headaches?

It's often said that farmers make the worst gardeners. It's true that folk who are used to tending hundreds of acres can't always manage to scale things down but overall, I'd say that Ambridge belies the notion. There are some wonderful gardens in the village and they represent the whole range of styles of English gardening, from the tiniest cottage plot to the grandest country house spread.

And so they should, because the soil in Ambridge is some of the best in the country. The deep, rich, brown, slightly acidic loam that makes such good pasture is equally effective at supporting gardens. The source of the rich brown colour is ironstone, and those with long memories might recall that there was once a suggestion that it should be mined locally. Fortunately, the plan never materialised.

The only outcrop of the underlying acid rock that I know of occurs on Lakey Hill, and that really does make for poor thin soil. Fortunately, no one gardens nearby. In truth, the only real problems come in those gardens closest to the Am where the soil tends to be lighter because of the overlying river alluvium which causes difficulties in hot summers as it dries out so quickly. But having the Stables and so many farms within everyone's reach, there's no shortage of that wonderful organic matter which helps moisture retention and structure on any type of soil.

Dear Stefan
As you doubtless know I'm very keen on aromatherapy, and I'd like to develop the gardens at the Hall as a source for my raw materials. Aromatherapy oils cost a fortune, and I'm sure that with a little application I can save a good deal of money by growing my own. Any suggestions?
Lynda Snell, Ambridge Hall

As I'm sure everyone knows, aromatherapy is the science and the art of using oils from aromatic plants to improve both beauty and health. I'm no aromatherapist, but I know that only natural ingredients will do; synthetic oils just don't work. And there are simply dozens and dozens of them: almost any aromatic plant has a use in aromatherapy. Unfortunately for Lynda, a very large number are not only tree-sized but also tropical. So, Lynda, unless you fancy putting up a very large, very warm conservatory at the Hall, you can forget about such glorious fragrances as ylang-ylang, sandalwood, cajeput and cinnamon.

And there's another problem. It's no good simply picking pieces of plant and rubbing them on your body. It's the oils that you need, and they have to be extracted by distillation, for which you need both a still and a licence. I'd hate to think of the local constabulary turning up on your doorstep. So I'd advise you to plant a selection of those aromatic oil plants that will grow in this country but use them just for decoration. You'll still have to buy your oils in bottles.

Almost all of the aromatic oil plants, like culinary herbs, come naturally from areas with a Mediterranean climate. They like maximum sunshine and a light, slightly alkaline soil. You'll be lucky to find much alkaline soil anywhere in Ambridge, but the light soil and sunny position of Ambridge Hall is otherwise ideal.

Herbal plants always look best in fairly formal beds, so I suggest that you construct a geometric layout of brick paths, dividing plots into smaller parts. You should try to match the lovely, mature West Midlands brick of the house but it's not a good idea to use real bricks as they will crack and crumble with frost. There are now some superb and fully durable replicas available for paving. They look wonderful arranged in herring-bone patterns.

Now for the plants themselves. I've listed plants that would be most reliable and I've grouped them by type, which reflects the way they should be grown. I've used both the aromatherapy names and also the scientific names.

CONIFERS (pruned to dwarf size)
Cade (*Juniperus oxycedrus*)
Cedarwood (*Cedrus libani atlantica*)
Cypress (*Cupressus sempervirens*)
Juniper (*Juniperus communis*)
Pine needle (*Abies sibirica*)

TENDER PLANTS to grow in pots and take under cover in winter or sown afresh each year
Geranium (*Pelargonium graveolens*)

Indian Basil (*Ocimum basilicum*)
Lemon grass (*Cymbopogon nardus*)
Tagetes (*Tagetes minuta*)

TALL PERENNIALS OR BIENNIALS
Angelica Root and Angelica Seed (*Angelica archangelica*)
Caraway (*Carum carvi*)
Carrot seed (*Daucus carota*)
Celery seed (*Apium graveolens*)
Coriander (*Coriandrum sativum*)
Dill seed (*Anethum graveolens*)
Fennel (*Foeniculum vulgare*)
Hops (*Humulus lupulus*)
Valerian root (*Valeriana officinalis*)

SHRUBS (or trees pruned as shrubs)
Bay (*Prunus laurocerasus*)
Eucalyptus (*Eucalyptus globulus*)
Jasmine (*Jasminum grandiflorum*)
Lavender (*Lavandula angustifolia*)
Rosemary (*Rosmarinus officinalis*)

SMALL PERENNIALS
German camomile (*Matricaria recutita*)
Peppermint (*Mentha x piperita*)
Roman camomile (*Anthemis nobilis*)
Sage clary (*Salvia sclarea*)
Spearmint (*Mentha spicata*)
Sweet marjoram (*Origanum majorana*)
Thyme (*Thymus serpyllum*)

Dear Stefan
My mother-in-law Doris Archer loved roses, and the ones she planted when Carol Tregorran re-planned the garden 40 years ago have all flourished. I'd like to add some roses too, sweet scented ones which flower several times a year to pass on for future generations. Suggestions please.
Jill Archer, Brookfield Farm

I think the perfect answer for Brookfield would be New English Roses. These have been bred in recent years by David Austin of Wolverhampton 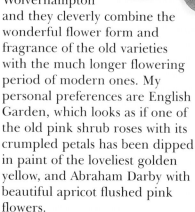 and they cleverly combine the wonderful flower form and fragrance of the old varieties with the much longer flowering period of modern ones. My personal preferences are English Garden, which looks as if one of the old pink shrub roses with its crumpled petals has been dipped in paint of the loveliest golden yellow, and Abraham Darby with beautiful apricot flushed pink flowers.

Dear Stefan
I do some part-time gardening for a lady who doesn't know a thing about it. I have to bite my tongue sometimes. How do you tell ignoramuses what gardening is all about?
Bert Fry, Woodbine Cottage

Take her into the garden with you Bert, put a small fork in her hand and start on some weeding together. Many people think I'm daft to say it, but hand weeding is the most wonderful way to learn to love gardening. You get down to the smell of the soil and a whole new world opens up to you.

Dear Stefan
We're converting one of the barns at Lower Loxley into an art gallery. We want it to look really swish. What plants do you recommend for inside? Will they be easy to look after or will we have to replace them at regular intervals? We're not that flush at the moment!
Nigel and Elizabeth Pargetter, Lower Loxley Hall

Although I've never been inside Lower Loxley (I'm still waiting for the invitation!) my guess is that the barn conversion will have fairly good light so that the visitors can see the pictures properly. But it will also be warm and dry. As you need big plants to make a statement, I would concentrate on the various forms of small leaved Ficus, like Ficus benjamina, the weeping fig. There are now some lovely variegated forms too. Keep them well watered and stand each pot in an outer container filled with pebbles in water. But whatever you do don't choose the large leaved rubber-plant type of Ficus; it will drop its leaves before you can say 'Mummy'.

Dear Stefan,
I'm doing a bit of regular gardening for an old lady in the village. I'd like to plant something nice but I don't know what. She's lived abroad a lot and I think she may like something to remind her of places she's been like Egypt or Kenya. Can anything truly exotic grow in our awful climate?
Neil Carter, No 1 The Green

The short is answer is yes, but not reliably. Tender plants may survive for a few years but the first really hard winter will flatten them. Global warming is only a part-time thing as far as gardeners are concerned. My advice is to choose things that look exotic but are really pretty tough. Try the sacred bamboo (*Nandina domestica*), the castor oil plant (*Fatsia japonica*), one or two New Zealand flax (*Phormium*) and a wonderful foliage shrub called *Fatshedera lizei*.

Dear Stefan
I'm on an economy kick, growing my own vegetables. I can manage carrots and sprouts. But someone told me to try something called kohl rabi. What exactly is it? And is really it as strange as it sounds?
Ruth Archer, Brookfield Farm

If you can grow sprouts Ruth, you can certainly grow kohl rabi. It's the one member of the brassica (cabbage) family that's never really caught on in Britain although it is very popular on the Continent. It looks like a cross between a turnip and a cabbage and should be sown directly into the growing positions in early summer. Space the plants about 25 cm apart and don't let the soil dry out. It has a lovely nutty, crunchy taste.

KNIT YOUR OWN

Archers Addicts Scarf

AS MODELLED BY EDDIE GRUNDY

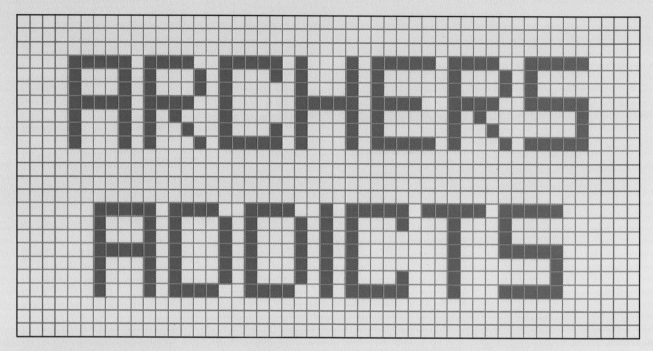

Everyone loves Eddie Grundy (Trevor Harrison) and everyone who meets her loves his Mum (Agnes Woolridge) too. We told Agnes that if she created a scarf for Archers Addicts we would let Eddie model it and she would get to keep the photograph. Agnes kindly fell into the trap, so now here's your chance to while away a couple of hours knitting. And then you can see if you measure up to Eddie. As far as his Mum's concerned that's downright impossible of course…

TO MAKE SCARF

LENGTH
153 cm

WOOL
Sirdar Prize double knitting in cream 300 grams
Sirdar Country Style double knitting in green 50 grams

NEEDLES
Number nine.

ABBREVIATIONS
K= knit
P= purl
St= stitch
Cm= centimetre
St.st.= stocking stitch (1 row knit, 1 row purl)
MS= main shade
C= colour

With number 9 needles, cast on 80 stitches.

First row: K3* P2, K2, repeat from * to last st, K1
Second row   K1* P2, K2, repeat from * to last 3 sts,
P2, K1

First and second rows form rib pattern.
Continue in rib until work measures 16 cms. Then start Archers Addicts logo.
6 rows 19 sts rib, 41 stocking st, rib 20 sts in MS

ADDICTS
See chart to count stitches for colour. 7 rows. 41 stocking st, alternating MS and C make up logo.
Rib 19 sts MS. Start stocking st. 2sts K MS, join in green wool for Addicts. 37 sts K alternating C and MS as chart, 2sts K MS, rib 20 sts MS.
Separate Addicts from Archers with 4 rows, 19 sts rib, 41 stocking st, rib 20 sts MS

ARCHERS
See chart to count stitches for colour. 7 rows.
Rib 19 sts MS. Start stocking st. for logo. Join in green wool for Archers. 41 sts K alternating C and MS as chart, rib 20 sts MS. 6 rows 19 sts rib, 41 stocking st, rib 20 sts in MS

Continue in rib MS for 121 cms. Reverse procedure for second logo starting with Archers first, then Addicts.
Rib MS for remaining 16 cms.

TO FINISH
Do not press. Sew all ends in neatly. Cut yarn into 30 cm. lengths and taking 4 strands together each time, knot along each short end to form a fringe. Trim fringes.

THE SNELLS OF AMBRIDGE HALL

What would Lynda Snell like to do for the New Millennium? Well, Lynda is convinced that she should be the new Mayor of Borsetshire: 'If London can have one, so should we.' Lynda can see herself in the flowing red robes with a cocked hat and a chain of office, standing on the balcony of the new Civic Centre waving to the crowds below as they welcome in the new century.

By the end of the year she will have sorted out the county's transport problems: every village will have a bus every 15 minutes, the trains will run on time and cars will be banned from the centres of Borchester and Felpersham. All domestic waste will be recycled or used in smokeless power stations, adding to the electricity supply generated by the wind turbines on Lakey Hill. Cycle lanes will be provided wherever they're needed. Local drama groups and music societies will be given the grants they need, subsidised by a tax on football. 'Borsetshire will be the envy of the world,' she declares. But first Lynda has to be elected.

Robert Snell is fully in agreement with Lyndie's plans. 'Yes, I'll be there to cheer in the New Millennium,' he says. But Robert will be thinking of all the committee meetings the Mayor will have to attend, all those lunches and dinners and overseas visits. Lynda's office will be in the new Civic Centre, which is such a long way from Ambridge Hall! How quiet it will be at home... Oh, peaceful New Millennium! Vote for Lynda Snell everyone!

MARJORIE AND HAYLEY IN NIGHTINGALE FARM

Circumstances threw Marjorie Antrobus and Hayley Jordan together at Nightingale Farm, but you'd be hard pushed to find two characters with less in common. Yet they've become firm friends – much to everyone's surprise. So will this odd couple be celebrating the Millennium together? Not on your life...

Marjorie will spend the evening quietly, looking back over the wealth of experience she's packed into a lifetime that's spanned most of the century. She'll think back to all those other New Year gatherings: the occasion in the Officers' Mess in Nairobi when a handsome young subaltern kept asking her to dance and Teddy threw a glass of champagne over him... The time they were coming home through the Suez Canal on New Year's Eve and were taken by camel across the desert to celebrations at the Sphinx and the Pyramids. Very romantic... And once, when they were out on safari, they sat round in a great circle and drank fermented elephants' milk from cups made from rhino horn. It was supposed to have some extraordinary effect, but Marjorie never discovered what it was... Then there was the very special night when she sat up waiting for one of her Afghan litters to be born; the first one emerged on the stroke of midnight. So many memories...

Hayley, meanwhile, will set off in her battered old car to a pre-arranged venue where she'll be greeted with shrieks of delight by a large group of friends. She'll spend the night on the dancefloor, and who knows what may happen? With Hayley's love of life, another romantic attachment can't be far away...

When she gets back to Nightingale Farm, Hayley will take a look to make sure that Marjorie is safe and sound in bed before kicking off her shoes and leaving a trail of clothes up the stairs.

Marjorie, who fell asleep listening to the shipping forecast on Radio 4, will turn over secure in the knowledge that the New Millennium has well and truly arrived at Nightingale Farm.

Diwali

FESTIVAL OF LIGHTS

WITH AUNTIE SATYA

Diwali – the Hindu festival of lights – is celebrated in Blossom Hill Cottage, Ambridge, each year. Usha Gupta brought the traditional Hindu celebration of colour, light and prosperity to the village, and every autumn – whatever the ups and downs that she's suffered in the preceding months – she gathers her family around her and prepares to light her lamps. Usha's mainstay throughout her sometimes troubled career in Ambridge has been her Auntie Satya, who visits each year to help out with the celebrations and to offer her niece a shoulder to cry on when necessary. So who better than Auntie Satya herself to take us through the rich and complex traditions that make up this highlight of *Archers* life?

'Every autumn, in October or November, we remember a great event from Hindu mythology – the return of Lord Rama, one of the major gods in our pantheon, from a long period of exile with his wife Sita. To welcome the couple home, their townsfolk lit strings of lamps, cleaned their homes and painted designs over the floors and walls – and these are the key elements of the celebrations today.

'Light is the main element of Diwali – the light that symbolises joy after grief, wisdom dispelling ignorance, and the spark of divine light within us all. Lighting a lamp, or *diva*, reminds us of the importance of bringing light and joy into other people's lives. The strings of lights at Diwali dispel the evils of hatred, poverty and sin, and act as an invitation to Lakshmi, the goddess of prosperity and good luck. We leave our doors open in the hope that she will come into our homes.

'Diwali also marks the end of the Hindu calendar and the financial year, so it's a time of reckoning and reconciliation as well as celebration. Everyone looks back and accounts for the work they've done in the last 12 months, praying for guidance to make the right decisions in the coming year. It's also a time to think about those who are less well off than ourselves; many people choose Diwali as an opportunity to give money to charity.

'In the evening, family and friends gather round the shrine at home for the prayers that form the focus of Diwali. Little statues of the gods are

The diva *is a lamp made of clay or metal with a cotton wick burning ghee (clarified butter)*

venerated inside the shrine, but the special focus at this time of year is the *puja* tray (puja means worship), something that we prepare with the utmost care in time for the lighting ceremony.'

Thanks to Usha Bahl for her help in compiling these pages.

A BELL
Rung to let the gods know prayers are about to begin.

INCENSE BURNER
To let sweet fragrances reach the gods.

AARTI LAMP
A metal diva lamp with five wicks, representing the five senses and the five elements.

OIL AND WICKS
For the divas

KUM KUM CONTAINER AND POWDER
The worshippers' foreheads and those of the statues are marked with red tilaka powder, bringing good health and prosperity.

YELLOW TURMERIC
To purify and cleanse.

WATER
Representing the sacred rivers of India, brings purity and life.

MILK
To wash the gods in the shrine.

FLOWERS, RICE, SWEETMEATS, FRUIT AND NUTS
Are offered as gifts to the gods.

'If anyone offers me with devotion
A leaf, flower, fruit, or water,
I accept that gift offered with devotion
From the giver who gives himself'

BHAGAVAD-GITA 9.26

Burfi Sweet

Burfi is the sweet eaten at special events and festivals such as Diwali. Last year I made trays and trays of burfi for the Ambridge Table Top Sale; everyone thought it tasted so delicious that I soon sold out. I passed the takings on to Lynda Snell! Here's my recipe: it's very simple to make, and delicious to eat.

Ingredients

8oz/230 grams dessicated coconut
1 large tin evaporated milk
8oz/230 grams caster sugar
30 fluid oz/1½ pints water
2 ½ oz/75 grams melted butter
Nuts, dried fruit and cardamom pods to decorate and flavour.

Method

Mix the coconut with the evaporated milk. Boil the sugar and water in a pan until it thickens. Lower the heat and add the coconut mix. Gradually add the melted butter, stirring continuously. Allow the mixture to thicken then add nuts, fruit or cardamom pods.

Spread the mixture onto a greased shallow tin. Let it cool for a few minutes, then mark into squares. Decorate with chopped nuts and leave to become completely cool and set before cutting or breaking into pieces.

Take a Walk

"Round about Lakey Hill – a man may walk as long as he will!"

(adapted from The Vision of Piers Plowman by William Langland)

Sometimes even the good people of Ambridge feel out of sorts: something to do with those long winter evenings and too many pints of Shires. So what better antidote to winter blues than a brisk walk around the village – with this handy rambler's guide.

The walk begins on Ambridge Village Green. If you arrive by car you can park around the Green, but be sure not to leave any valuables visible.

With the duck pond on your left, set off past Honeysuckle Cottage on the road to the right signposted 'Borchester'. Rehearsals for the pantomime may be in progress in what was once the local school and is now the village hall, on your left. Keep going and you're soon out of the village.

Ignore the strong smell of pigs as you go past a farm track on your right. Immediately on your left is the tree-lined drive leading to the now disused Arkwright Hall. There's an optional detour here if you're interested in seeing what remains of this ancient edifice, parts of which are said to date from the 17th century, but don't expect an architectural masterpiece. Pevsner describes it as 'a real mish-mash of styles, one of those buildings best forgotten', and any claims that Arkwright Hall has links with the inventor of the spinning jenny can be dismissed as pure supposition. It does boast a priest hole, however, discovered in 1959.

Returning to the road, turn left towards Borchester and note the fine hawthorn hedges on both sides of the road. These were nearly scrubbed up a few years ago but were saved by public outcry, and now they are cut back by hand each year in the traditional way.

FROM THIS POINT YOU CAN HEAR JOE GRUNDY GRUMBLING

Ahead, on the left, near a large oak tree, you will see a sign to Ambridge cricket ground. Rather quiet in the winter months, but in the summer the sound of leather on willow can be heard from the road, as can the more vocal appeals to the umpire.

Continue to a block paved drive on the right, leading to barn conversions with their characteristic café rods and lace curtains. Despite what anyone may tell you there is a public right of way down this lane, and the Borsetshire County Council has promised to restore the public footpath sign. It is clearly marked on the Ordnance Survey map.

Once past the barns, turn right and follow the footpath along a sparse hedge round a field of winter wheat. Follow the footpath round to the left and start climbing Lakey Hill.

This famous landmark rises to 771 feet above sea level and is said to be the site of several pre-historic burial mounds. Although part of Brookfield Farm, and owned by the Archer family, the top of Lakey Hill remains open to the public and has given pleasure to many generations. Commemorative bonfires light up the hill on festive occasions.

From the summit you can follow the line of the River Am and see the tributaries flowing into it. On a clear day looking south you can just make out the high-rise flats in Felpersham, and to the west the churches of Borchester stand out against the setting sun. Looking down into Ambridge it's easy to pick out the individual houses. If it's quiet you may hear a skylark high above you. Forty years ago there were flocks of skylarks above Lakey Hill, but now you are lucky to hear one or two.

Take care coming down the South side of the hill, as the descent is steep and, if there has been rain, slippery. Some of you may remember the fun that was had here with the Easter egg rolling race. At the bottom you emerge on to a well-used lane which leads around Willow Farm. In summer you may be tempted by the pick-your-own strawberries available here. Once past the farm turn right onto the track leading to the main road.

Be careful how you cross the road as there have been several nasty accidents on this stretch in recent bends to the right and flows into shallow reed beds. Years ago, gypsies harvested the reeds to make baskets, which they sold at Borchester market. Now the reeds provide a safe home for the moorhens and coots which frequent this part of the river. The ducks and swans are more gregarious and you'll find them near the bridge hoping to be fed. Watch out for water voles on the opposite bank; they live in burrows along the river, but are likely to dive if they see you coming.

When you reach the smaller of the village's two

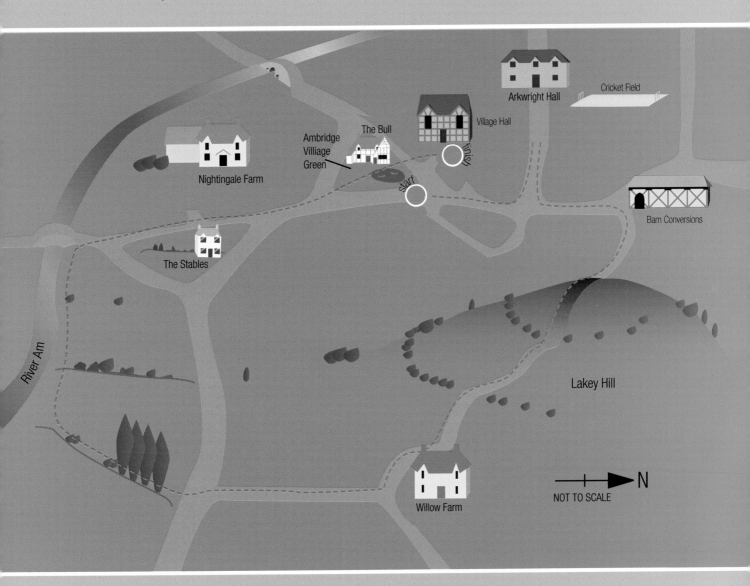

years. Ahead you'll see a footpath leading towards four poplar trees. Go over the stile and follow the footpath to the river Am.

The footpath sign points to the right, and you follow the course of the river along the bank until it bridges, return to the road with Nightingale Farm on the left and The Stables on the right until you find yourself back on the Green again. Should you then be in need of refreshment, Sid and Kathy Perks in The Bull will be pleased to serve you.

computer

Computer dating? It happens in Ambridge every day. Individual details are processed by a special programme that matches the perfect female to the perfect male, to make sure that the next generation is genetically perfect. So far, this sinister practice is limited to the bovine world — but what would happen if humans, as well as cattle, could take advantage of the service? We'd certainly see some very different pairings among the good people of Ambridge.

We've asked local computer whizz and IT expert Robert Snell to help us with a one-off experiment in social engineering. We put 14 names into the computer — seven women and seven men — and let the programme do its worst. Here are the results.

FEMALES

Name: **Lynda Snell**
Age: **52**
Status: **Married**
Occupation: **Receptionist/Administrator at Grey Gables Hotel.**
Interests: **Bicycles, campaigns, theatre, dogs, goats.**
Robert's view: **Lyndie is wonderfully artistic, sensitive to a fault and takes a keen interest in village affairs.**

Name: **Hayley Jordan**
Age: **22**
Status: **Single**
Occupation: **Nanny.**
Interests: **Pig breeding, children.**
Robert's view: **Brummie blonde with a soft spot for Old Spots.**

Name: **Pat Archer**
Age: **47**
Status: **Married**
Occupation: **Farmer, entrepreneur.**
Interests: **Organic farming, women's rights, *The Guardian*.**
Robert's view: **Middle-aged and mellow. Her ideas may be feminist but her ice cream is absolutely delicious.**

Name: **Caroline Pemberton**
Age: **44**
Status: **Rich widow**
Occupation: **Manager of Grey Gables Hotel.**
Interests: **White-water rafting, animals, classical music. A keen horsewoman.**
Robert's view: **Caroline needs someone who can handle her delightful elegance, sophistication and style. If my hands weren't full with Lyndie...**

MALES

Name: **John Higgs**
Age: **60s**
Status: **Single**
Occupation: **Jack Woolley's chauffeur.**
Interests: **Prize-winning chrysanthemums, dogs, playing pantomime dame.**
Robert's view: **The strong silent type.**

Name: **Tony Archer**
Age: **48**
Status: **Married**
Occupation: **Organic farmer.**
Interests: **Foreign holidays, drinking, pulling leeks (in moderation).**
Robert's view: **He can certainly pull the leeks, but can he pull the ladies? We shall see.**

Name: **Brian Aldridge**
Age: **55**
Status: **Married**
Occupation: **Farmer, Director of Borchester Land.**
Interests: **Shooting, fishing.**
Robert's view: **I cannot fathom the undoubted attraction he has for the opposite sex. Women need to look out.**

Name: **Tim Hathaway**
Age: **30s**
Status: **Married**
Occupation: **GP.**
Interests: **Country life.**
Robert's view: **Something of an enigma.**

mating

Name: Peggy Woolley
Age: **75**
Status: **Twice married**
Occupation: **Helps out in hotel when short-staffed.**
Interests: **Cats, ballroom dancing.**
Robert's view: **A touch old-fashioned, the tiniest hint of blue hair rinse. She says she's no romantic, but Cary Grant would make her sigh.**

Name: Betty Tucker
Age: **49**
Status: **Married**
Occupation: **Manager of the village shop and post office**
Interests: **Her grand-daughter, the WI.**
Robert's view: **Betty's a good woman and has a hard time with her husband, Mike, so she deserves a treat. Potential suitors should be prepared to wine and dine.**

Name: Tracy Horrobin
Age: **24**
Status: **Single**
Occupation: **Ex-Bridge Farm temporary dairy supervisor, now barmaid at the Cat and Fiddle.**
Interests: **Acting, men in general.**
Robert's view: **Passionate, cute, great fun to be with – or so I've heard.**

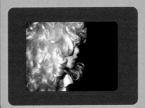

HERE ARE THE COMPUTER PAIRINGS – AND WHAT OUR NEW COUPLES THINK OF EACH OTHER

John – I'd drive Mrs Snell to the moon and back. She only has to ask.
and
Lynda – He's already driving me crazy.

Hayley – Well, Tony's tried his best but I've given up pigs!
and
Tony – Hayley can pull my leeks any time.

Pat – It's Brian who put the suffer in 'suffragette'.
and
Brian – I've never thought of Pat in that way , but now I come to look at her…

Caroline – I'll take the medicine like a good girl.
and
Tim – Just what the doctor ordered!.

Jack – Peggy's got a special place in my heart.
and
Peggy – Jack's the one for me!

Sid – Great news! Shires on the house!
and
Betty – The Shires may be free but I'm not, so I'll have to pass. Sorry Sid.

Tracy – Ooh yummy! He's gorgeous! I could eat him for breakfast.
and
Roy – Have I bitten off more than I can chew?

Name: Jack Woolley
Age: **80**
Status: **Twice married**
Occupation: **Proprietor of the *Borchester Echo*, owner of Grey Gables.**
Interests: **Gadgets, dogs, ballroom dancing, strawberry tartlets.**
Robert's view: **One of nature's gentlemen. Romantic and generous – the lady of his choice will be treated like a queen.**

Name: Sid Perks
Age: **55**
Status: **Twice married**
Occupation: **Co-owner of The Bull.**
Interests: **Ambridge Cricket Club, keeping fit, tinkering with cars.**
Robert's view: **Sid's looking very muscular these days. Certainly fit enough to take on the fair sex.**

Name: Roy Tucker
Age: **21**
Status: **Unmarried father**
Occupation: **University student, waiter at Grey Gables.**
Interests: **Aston Villa FC, music.**
Robert's view: **Anyone who is the father of Kate Aldridge's child and cheerfully attends her new age ceremonies deserves respect.**

The Gloves

Under different circumstances, they might have been best friends. But as it is, Hayley Jordan and Helen Archer are squaring up for one of the biggest catfights in the history of Ambridge. But before you place your bets on the outcome, take a look at our handy guide to their past form – and get the inside story from some of the people who know them best

On your left, the Brummie Bruiser

Hayley Jordan
Age: 22
Background: City girl, came to Ambridge as a nanny.
Character: Outgoing, likeable, resourceful, always willing to lend a hand. Honest to a fault.

History

- Hayley met John Archer – Helen's brother – and they fell in love, set up home together in April Cottage and planned to live happily ever after.
- All went well until Hayley discovered that John was two-timing with his old flame Sharon Richards. Hayley walked out and refused to have anything more to do with him.
- Repentant John begged Hayley's forgiveness, and finally resorted to proposing marriage. Still upset, Hayley threw the ring back in his face – something she regretted bitterly the next day, when John was killed in a farming accident.
- Grieving Hayley was left looking after John's organically reared pigs. Fortunately, John's younger brother Tommy was at hand to help out, and the business took off.
- The Ambridge gossips started to wonder if Tommy would pick up where John had left off – but so far nothing has come of their

relationship other than simple friendship.
- Hayley moved into Ambridge to be near her work, and now she rents a flat from Mrs Antrobus at Nightingale Farm.
- Hayley and Tommy's pig business flourished, and they launched their very own organic pork and leek sausages, Ambridge Originals, to an enthusiastic market.
- All was going well until Helen Archer returned to Ambridge hell-bent on undermining Hayley's position in the family. Questioning Hayley's motives and making her feel like an interloper, she finally squeezed her out of the business.
- Encouraged by Helen, Tony told Hayley that she couldn't be a partner in the sausage business. Hayley stormed out to concentrate on being a nanny. And as long as Helen has any say in the matter, it looks like she won't be coming back.

are Off

On your right, the Bridge Farm Hellcat

Helen Archer
Age: 20
Background: Ambridge born and bred. A student of Reaseheath Agricultural College.
Character: Selfish, bossy, cool-headed, practical. Single-minded in pursuit of revenge.

History

- In her teens Helen was a member of the notorious Blossom Hill Cottage Gang, led by her cousin Kate Aldridge, with whom she spent many a happy hour smoking, drinking cider and reading lonely hearts columns.
- Helen left Ambridge (and the distracting influence of Kate) to study dairy management at Reaseheath.
- When brother John was killed, Helen quickly returned to college – and is left with a feeling of guilt and unresolved grief.
- Helen returned to Bridge Farm determined to modernise working practices in the dairy.
- She was furious when she discovered that Hayley had taken over John's pigs – and drawn little brother Tommy into the business as well! Helen was convinced that Hayley's motives were selfish: she'd worm her way into the

family's affections and eventually get her hands on the Archer inheritance.
- She hatched a plan to oust Hayley from the business, claiming that the pork sales were part of Bridge Farm's output and undermining sausage sales with her superior grasp of marketing.
- Despite Tommy's insistence that he and Hayley were equal partners, Helen persuaded her parents that she could never be more than an employee.
- Determined to keep Hayley out, Helen deferred her placement to Zimbabwe and went to work with Anne Baxter, a specialist cheese maker in Borchester.
- It's not all going Helen's way, however. Her attempts to modernise the dairy during her mother's illness failed, and her decision to appoint Tracy Horrobin as her supervisor (overseeing Clarrie Grundy and Colin Kennedy) backfired badly.

Brothers and Lovers

Hayley and Helen have a great deal in common: not least a shared bond with the three main men in their lives

TOMMY ARCHER

JOHN ARCHER

ROY TUCKER

HAYLEY: He was my business partner, but more than that, he was a good pal and confidant. We've been through mud, sweat and tears together.

HELEN: Tom will be fine if he just does as I say and gets away from Hayley's influence.

TOMMY: I'll always feel guilty about what happened with the partnership deal with Hayley. We were doing fine until Helen interfered. Sisters really are a pain in the neck. I know exactly what I'm doing. I don't need any advice, not from Mum or Dad and certainly not from Helen.

HAYLEY: The only drawback was that to love John you had to love his pigs! But I didn't mind. Quite simply, John was the love of my life. I know he was no angel, but I miss him.

HELEN: We got on okay as long as we were apart! Perhaps because we were too alike – go-getting, headstrong, demanding. Like Mum, I guess. But I think he's the only member of my family who'd understand what I've been trying to do with the marketing. He could have given me some tips on how to handle Tommy as well. Whether you get on with a brother or not, you miss them like heck when they're not around.

HAYLEY: Roy's a good friend. He tried to get John and me together again after we split up and he was a great shoulder to cry on. Especially after John died. And he knows I'm there for him too, and he let me help Kate and him sort out their differences over Phoebe. He's different from John and I don't think he's as good-looking, but he's really nice. Bit of a boy-nextdoor. He'll kill me for saying that!

HELEN: He's a hunk. I could definitely fancy him!

ROY: A couple of feisty females. I'd take them both on, if they gave me the chance.

fact file

NAME: DAVID THOMAS ARCHER
BORN: 18 September 1959
ADDRESS: Brookfield Farm, Ambridge
OCCUPATION: Partner in Brookfield Farm with wife Ruth, and parents Phil and Jill
FAMILY: Married to farmer Ruth. One daughter Philippa Rose, 'Pip' (born 1993), and one son Joshua (born 1997)
HOBBIES: Cricket
SINS: Jackie Woodstock, Sophie Barlow, fast cars, big tractors

HIGHS

1980 Qualifies from the Royal Agricultural College, Cirencester, to his great relief.

1988 Becomes a fully fledged director of Ambridge Farmers Ltd. Makes it to the altar at last, with agricultural student Ruth Pritchard.

1991 David and Ruth move into the new bungalow built especially for them at Brookfield. Phil offers David and Ruth 60% of Brookfield profits.

1993 Daughter Pip is born in Borchester General.

1997 David interrupts a vital cricket match to ensure that he's present at the birth of son Joshua – and is hit for six by the result.

1999 David and Ruth move into Brookfield and take over the running of the farm. The herd is finally cleared of TB.

LOWS

1977 Fails his Maths 'A' level retake because of his infatuation for glamorous sheep-shearer, Michele Brown.

1986 Lisping dress designer Sophie Barlow cancels their wedding.

1987 Blames himself for the accidental death of Jethro Larkin while tree-cutting.

1998 TB is found in the Brookfield herd. Cattle slaughtered to prevent the disease spreading.

What if...
Jethro's tragic accident had not taken place?
Phil would not have employed a student to take his place and David would never have met Ruth.

Timothy Bentinck

Timothy Bentinck was born on a Tasmanian sheep station. Returning to England when he was two, the family sent Timothy to Harrow; he continued his studies at the University of East Anglia and the Bristol Old Vic Theatre School. Timothy got a six-month contract with the radio Drama Rep, with an Equity Card to boot; shortly thereafter, Ambridge called. Now he divides his time between *The Archers* and a career in voice-overs, as well as TV work (*By the Sword Divided*, *Boon*, *Grange Hill*).

Timothy and his wife, Judith, live in a Victorian semi in Islington which they modernised themselves, with their sons William and Jasper.

If there's one thing that's harder than being a farmer in Ambridge, it's being the son of a farmer. Ask David Archer. He's finally taking over the reins of Brookfield Farm, but still has his parents looking over his shoulder. It's a difficult position for a man of 40 to put up with.

The handover would never have taken place had it not been for Jill's knee injury, which forced her and Phil to slow down and take stock of their future. In theory they're now taking more of a back seat while David and Ruth look after the business, occasionally chipping in with a bit of well-meant advice. In practice, though, it's just not going to be as straightforward as that.

David has been involved in work at Brookfield since his grandfather Dan was still alive, and saw for himself the problems created when two or more generations try to work together. But he's inherited Phil's quick temper, and doesn't always learn from the lessons of the past. Things were made worse when he married Ruth, a graduate of Harper Adams College fully conversant with modern farming methods and eager to apply them as an equal partner in the running of Brookfield. Jill in particular found this hard to handle: after being a traditional farmer's wife for all of her married life, she found it hard to come to terms with a daughter-in-law who seemed determined to have things her way. The arrival of Pip and Josh poured oil on troubled waters, though, and David was delighted when Phil finally invited Ruth to become a partner in the farm.

The past year has been a difficult one for David and Ruth. Many of the enlarged herd became infected with TB, Ruth blamed herself for bringing the infected cows into Brookfield, and Phil fought down the temptation to say 'I told you so'. And with money tighter than ever, the Archers had to cut back on personal spending – with all the ensuing rows.

David reluctantly sacrificed his beloved four-wheel drive, and Ruth turned her energies to growing their own vegetables. Now they're eating some of their own meat from the slaughterhouse; more work than buying it from the butcher, but cheaper than ready-made meals. But every cloud has a silver lining: David has developed a particularly fine line in Shepherd's Pie.

Tightening belts at home has been fairly successful, then: but economies on the farm were much harder to impose. Luckily, David's been able to avoid costly vets' bills by applying his own expertise to the stock's various ailments. But times are still tough, and careful management will be needed if Brookfield is to thrive into the next century. Whatever David decides will have enormous repercussions: this, after all, is the man who's raising the next generation of Archers.

RELATIVE VALUES

Stephen Fry, long-lost cousin of Ambridge's own poet-in-residence Bert Fry, has undertaken a labour of love compiling *The Archers* Crossword. Here he fills us in on his years away from Ambridge

Stephen Fry is the Jacob's sheep of the Fry family: unlike his cousin Bert, with whom *Archers* listeners will be familiar, Stephen left the warm nourishing bosom of the Borsetshire countryside at an early age to seek his fortune in the false, lurid glare of London.

Occasionally he writes to Bert, but only to beg for money to help finance one or other of his disreputable schemes, which have included pretending to be Oscar Wilde in the film *Wilde* and playing Jeeves in *Jeeves and Wooster* (an excuse to meet Graham Seed, Jack May and Mary Wimbush – Nigel, Nelson and Julia) as well as writing books called *Paperweight* and his autobiography *Moab is My Washpot*.

Stephen hopes one day to be rich and famous enough to be asked to open a fête at Ambridge. Until that time he keeps abreast of village news as much as he can. He once met Shane in a tapas bar in Notting Hill and is one of a small band that believes Cameron Fraser was greatly misunderstood.

Answers on page 96

Across

1   Gamboling lambs he makes shuffle along (7).
5   Vessel returns to vessel's return – could be a request (3-4).
9   Borsetshire council running the 3? (5,10).
10   To begin with Mrs Antrobus uprooted dahlias for her (4).
11   Lynda's back in woollen sock (5).
12   In pig, any number likely to fall in winter (4).
15   A nocturnal charge for fertiliser, we hear (7).
16   Webster's handwriting like this? (7).
17   He destroyed romance! (7).
19   Ripens around archdeacon and requites (7).
21   Bad ones take a long time (4).
22   Share soup with farm animals (5).
23   Notes in the land of Nod (4).
26   Archer put in Latin for one of these – 3 as well (4,2,3,6).
27   Skater's Waltz on the tractor wheels? (7).
28   Coupled side with real meaning (7).

Down

1   The shortest-lived member of the Grundy family? (7).
2   Story editor? In fact he's in charge of the books (8,7).
3   Perks up here? Rubbish! (4).
4   Utter, utter nonsense of EC involvement in various French and English units (7).
5   Projects the sound of a pop-group (7).
6   Carol is up to no good (4).
7   In Islington Nelson found a divine messenger! (3, 5, 7).
8   Imprison set-aside (3,4).
13   See one in fat land-owner (5).
14   Seed came back to replay him (5).
17   Farmhouse and cottage made up these (7).
18   Scores with books concealed in the buttocks (7).
19   They should take a bow! (7).
20   Cardies snagged on the passenger seat (7).
24   Oddly froglike people (4).
25   Milkmaid bore it adequately in the old surroundings (4).

Julia
has all the answers

Julia Pargetter: actress, novelist, businesswoman. Widow, mother and recovering alcoholic. A woman who has taken on the world and returned triumphant. Who better than the lady of Lower Loxley Hall, the author of Passion's Plaything, to offer pearls from her store of wisdom to her troubled fellow villagers?

UNABLE TO COPE

I'm finding it very hard to come to terms with the death of my son nearly two years ago in a farm accident. For a while I was completely unable to cope, which led me to have a breakdown. I've recovered from that, but despite having another son, a daughter and a loving husband, the loss still hangs over me. P.A.

Losing a dear one is something that happens to us all. I know that doesn't make it any easier, but you do have to face up to it. Look around you and you'll find many others in a far worse situation than yourself. Be glad that you have other children and a loving husband to share your grief. It may not be so evident as in your case, but they are probably still suffering too.

LOOKING FOR A GENT

What hope is there for me – a successful businesswoman in my 40s? I was married to a charming gentleman who sadly died three years ago. Since then I seem to meet men who are boring and self-centred with no idea of how to treat a lady. I've tried answering dating advertisements, but that was a farce. Have you or your readers any better ideas? C.P.

You must just be looking for the wrong sort of man. As a successful businesswoman myself I come up against attractive men in all walks of life. We even had some builders in who knew exactly how to treat a lady. Remember the old adage: 'A lady is a woman who allows a man to be a gentleman.'

MOPES AROUND THE HOUSE

I dearly love my second husband and with his work as a gamekeeper and mine running a riding stables our time together was limited, but precious. But now that he's retired he doesn't know what to do with himself. He mopes around the house all day and keeps asking for "things to do". I don't wish to upset him but I have got my work to get on with. C.B.

Yours is a common problem, but as with other milestones in life you have to learn to adjust. Encourage him in his hobbies; leave your work for a while and go out for a pub lunch together. His retirement should mean greater pleasures for you. Try teaching the old dog some new tricks!

BRIEF FLING

When I first landed my present job I thought I was on a winner. To be a land agent meant I was working on my own and taking my responsibilities seriously. After I failed to repossess a farm I thought was being badly run I realised I was being cold shouldered by my neighbours. I had a brief fling with a lady friend but it came to

nothing. *I may be tired of living in the country, I just don't know. Should I pack it in now, or stick it out in the hope that something and someone more rewarding will come along? G.R.*

You must be true to yourself, dear boy. If you are bored with the country then it obviously doesn't suit you. You could try a job in town. You'd soon discover the change in your environment will bring a change to your love life. Give fate a nudge. Good luck.

FISH OUT OF WATER

I am the first member of my family to go to university and to tell the truth I feel like a fish out of water. Most of my fellow students come from fairly well-off families, whereas I have problems coping with my tuition fees and my keep, and have to work long hours. I am also worried about the mother of my child and our small baby, especially as our relationship fell apart. My parents are supportive but I don't think they understand what I am going through. Am I alone in this situation? R.T.

No, of course you aren't. Universities are full of people from widely varying backgrounds who are all having money problems even if they don't tell you they are. Your girlfriend has undergone a very traumatic experience and wants to prove that she can manage on her own. Perservere: go and see her when you are next home. She may need to talk to you now. And R.T., parents have never ever understood what their children are going through.

TIME FOR CHANGE?

I came to Borsetshire several years ago. My partner and I spent a lot of time and money turning a grotty old pub into a smart venue with a first-class restaurant. We've built up a really good business, but my partner feels that we should own our own premises, not rent from the brewery as we do now. We did make tentative enquiries about another local establishment, but it wasn't available for sale. My partner suggests looking further afield, but I'm reluctant to leave the area. What should we do? S.M.

Are you sure your partner hasn't got itchy feet for another reason? We own our premises (I have for centuries in fact) and it does seem to be nothing but trouble. Why not stick it out for a bit longer – or just bide your time until something local becomes available.

BARRIER GRIEF

I am not in the habit of writing to a problem page, but I am at a loss to know how to proceed. Try as I may, I can't seem to get through to my husband. I know he has problems with his business but there seems to be a barrier between us. Our eldest daughter has a close relationship with him, but I feel left out in the cold. J.A.

I assume from your letter that you are tending towards middle age?

Many women at this stage begin to see problems where none really exists. Go and see your GP. He or she may be able to prescribe something to help you through the difficult times.

Julia Pargetter

+IEALTH WISE

WITH DR HATHAWAY

In the months since I took over the practice, I've learnt a great deal about the health of a rural community, and a fascinating study it has proved to be.

I'm interested that so many of you still swear by the old remedies, although I have to say that getting rid of warts by rubbing them with the inside of a broad bean pod or stroking a sty nine times with a gold wedding ring, is not what I'd recommend.

Doctors always boast that there's no quicker route to the heart of a community than through the GP's surgery, and I've certainly learnt a good deal about Ambridge and the folk that live here since I arrived. Here's a selection from my recent postbag.

TAKE 'EM AWAY

I'm fed up with being called 'pizza face' by my friends at school because of my spotty face. My elder brother sold me some stuff to put on them, which he made himself, but that's just made them worse. What can I do?
Edward Grundy, Grange Farm.

Dr H: Throw it away!

AROMATHERAPY IN BAD ODOUR?

In common with most doctors you have fallen into a common trap. Not once have you mentioned aromatherapy. Extraordinary when you consider how many people are helped by *eau de lavande* and *huile de geranium*. Please remedy this immediately and give your views on this overlooked school of medicine (practised by witch doctors and wise women long before modern medicine was even thought of...)
Lynda Snell, Ambridge Hall.

Dr H: Practice makes perfect, but we've got a long way to go yet!

SEEN BUT NOT HEARD

I work as receptionist at a very posh hotel in Ambridge. You'd think that people would notice me but they never do. It's like I don't exist or something. The only time I got a bit of attention was when I played a part in the local panto, but now everything's back to normal. What's wrong with me?
Trudy Porter, Grey Gables.

Dr H: It's all in your imagination.

FARMER'S LUNG: FACT OR FICTION?

For years I've been a terrible sufferer from Farmer's Lung. It's worse if I get up too early in the mornings or work on too late at nights. I often wish I could help my son and his lovely wife more but I'm crippled with this hacking cough. Now the doctor says there's no such thing and refuses to give me my special mixture until he's given me a check up. He must think I'm a hippocratic or something. Can I ask for a second opinion?
Joseph Grundy, Grange Farm

Dr H: Yes.

So You Think You're an Addict?

You can't stop thinking about it. You talk about it all the time. Your friends and family are mystified; colleagues can't understand half of what you're saying. You become nervous and excited at regular times every day, but doctors can find nothing physically wrong with you. You are one of millions across the country suffering from (or should that be rejoicing in?) a condition that's been spreading since 1951. You are an Archers Addict. Find out just how bad it really is with our special quiz, carefully devised to sort out the true addicts from the casual fans.

1 Eddie Grundy's turkeys are a scraggy bunch at the best of times. How does he stop his turkeys pecking one another?
a Paints them with a tar-like substance
b Plays them 'Barwick Green'
c Hangs an old cabbage in their living quarters

2 Where did Martha think ghostly Florrie Hoskins used to live before she drowned herself in the village pond?
a Blossom Hill Cottage
b Nightingale Farm
c April Cottage

3 Who owns the freehold of The Bull?
a Peggy Woolley
b Shires Brewery
c Sid Perks and Caroline Pemberton

4 What part did Baggy and Snatch play in *Jack and the Beanstalk*?
a The Broker's Men
b Claribelle the Cow
c Snatch'em and Bag'em

5 Who composed the *Archers* signature tune, 'Barwick Green'?
a Arthur Wood
b Henry Wood
c Victoria Wood

6 On which festive day did Shula and Alistair marry?
a Christmas Eve
b Boxing Day
c New Year's Day

7 Hayley Jordan performed a memorable monologue on Red Nose Day at The Bull. What was it called?
a My First Introduction to the Countryside
b Everyone Loves a Sausage
c What a Red Nose Means to Me

8 Where did Mrs Antrobus live immediately before she came to Ambridge?
a Battersea
b Waterley Cross
c Kenya

9 What rank did dashing Freddie Danby hold when he was in the Army?
a Captain
b Sergeant
c Colonel

10 Poor David had to economise. What did he sell?
a His 4-wheel drive
b His body
c His fertiliser spreader

11 Feet walking through bracken – a familiar sound to listeners. How do you think it's made?
a Treading on egg shells
b Crunching mangled recording tape underfoot
c Real bracken

12 What is gorgeous Country & Western star Jolene's real name?
a Lily
b Nolene
c Doreen

13 Where is Kenton sowing his wild oats now?
a New Zealand
b Australia
c Budleigh Salterton

14 Where was the stable fire that killed Grace?
a Grey Gables
b Ambridge Hall
c Brookfield

15 What is Julia Pargetter's bodice-ripping novel called?
a Passion's Plaything
b Evangeline
c Take a Pair of Turquoise Eyes

16 What will be the episode number of *The Archers* broadcast on 1 January 2000?
a 10,097
b 200,023
c 74,650

17 Where in Birmingham were the first episodes of *The Archers* recorded?
a Albert Square
b Broad Street
c Gosta Green

18 Who is the odd man out?
a Jack May
b Chris Gittins
c Robert Mawdsley

19 What solid-fuel stove provides warmth in the kitchen at Grange Farm?
a Aga
b Saga
c Rayburn

20 The women of Ambridge have always been handy with a needle and thread. What impressive example of their work hangs in St Stephen's church?
a An embroidered crest of the Lawson Hope family
b A communion cloth
c A peace quilt

21 What was Dan Archer's mother's name?
a Phoebe
b Doris
c Danielle

22 How far is it from Ambridge to Felpersham?
a 6 miles
b 10 miles
c 17 miles

23 Last year's panto, *Jack and the Beanstalk*, was a hit with its audiences. But what was unusual about the cast?
a None of them lived in Ambridge
b None of them has ever been heard on the programme
c None of them has ever appeared with the Ambridge Players before

24 How many acres of farmland does Brookfield Farm have?
a 469
b 513
c 1,523

25 There was a sigh of relief when the villainous Simon Pemberton disappeared from Borsetshire. Where did he go?
a Brazil
b Dubai
c Costa Brava

26 Jack thought Peggy looked a million dollars when she modelled in the Over-60s fashion show. What did he buy for her?
a The high-heeled shoes she wore on the catwalk
b A revealing blouse
c A shimmery dress

27 By what surname has Shula decided that her son Daniel should be known?
a Hebden
b Lloyd-Archer
c Archer-Hebden

28 Kathy likes to leap to the rescue. To which voluntary organisation does she belong?
a Samaritans
b St John's Ambulance
c Red Cross

29 Where in *Radio Times* does the cast list of *The Archers* appear? (no cheating!)
a On the Friday Radio 4 page
b On the Radio Review page
c After the Sunday omnibus edition

30 Where was Usha Gupta born?
a Sri Lanka
b Uganda
c Birmingham

NOW CHECK YOUR SCORE:
Score THREE points for each correct answer.

1 c
2 c
3 c *(Peggy sold the freehold to Sid Perks and Guy Pemberton. Guy bequeathed his interest to Caroline)*
4 b
5 a
6 a
7 a
8 b
9 c
10 a
11 b
12 c
13 b
14 a *(Phil and Grace were having dinner there when they saw the fire.)*
15 a
16 A trick question! *The Archers* isn't broadcast on a Saturday.
17 b
18 a *(The other two actors played Walter Gabriel)*
19 c
20 c
21 a
22 c
23 b
24 a
25 b
26 c
27 a
28 b
29 a
30 b

IF YOU SCORED:

0-30 You'd do well to stay in bed on a few Sunday mornings and catch up on the omnibus edition. While you're at it, phone your mother and pick her brains about the show.

31-64 You're a potential addict. You're listening, yes – but are you really paying attention? Are you being distracted, perhaps by food or work? Don't you know of a quiet room where you can take your radio and listen without interruptions?

65-90 Congratulations: you're addicted. Admit it: you sometimes listen to the same episode twice, with increased enjoyment. You own tapes of *Vintage Archers,* and you have a special Addict-friend who you phone up to discuss the week's events.

Kate Aldridge

Libra 23 September to 22 October

STAR QUALITIES: Loves people. Can be good natured and pleasant, but can also turn sulky and balk at taking orders.
DISTINGUISHING FEATURE: Dimples (dimple in chin, devil within!)
LUCKY COLOUR: Pastel blue.
LUCKY STONES: Diamond, opal.
LOVE: You're a whole lotta woman for a man who's interested in romance.
MONEY: Plentiful amounts of money are needed to lift you out of your current surroundings.
HEALTH: Guard against over-indulgence. It brings you out in spots.
WORK: Business problems will be quickly solved with the help of your amazing powers of analysis.
FAMOUS LIBRANS: Mahatma Gandhi, Oscar Wilde, Grace Archer, Dwight Eisenhower.

Daniel Hebden

Scorpio 23 October to 22 November

STAR QUALITIES: Scorpio has a magnetic personality which immediately attracts others and subjects them to his strong will. Loves a mystery.
LUCKY COLOUR: Black.
SCORPIO TRAITS: Piercing eyes of hypnotic intensity.
GUARD AGAINST: The fascination of fire.
LOVE: You can take any amount of love and affection and are filled with boundless loyalty to friends and loved ones.
HEALTH: You have a miraculous ability to withstand pain. Could be prone to nose bleeds or an accident during sport.
WORK: Wise beyond your years, you are determined to get what you want and strong enough to hang on to it. You dream of being a space engineer, fireman, government minister or even prime minister.
FAMOUS SCORPIOS: Pablo Picasso, Prince Charles, Tom Forrest, Marie Antoinette.

Mike Tucker

Sagittarius 23 November to 21 Decemb

STAR QUALITIES: Honest and true. Trustworthy and a natural teacher. A little rebellious just for the sake of it. Animal lover.
LUCKY COLOUR: Turquoise.
LOVE: A big hearted gambler, willing to take a chance on love but difficult to catch. Sagittarians never grow up.
MONEY: You're generous about spending money, but you should always stick to the truth: don't try deception.
HEALTH: Give in to sickness reluctantly - recuperate swiftly. Beware your love of food and drink. Think moderation.
WORK: You're lucky: most of your messes turn out all right. Exhilarated by speed, danger.
FAMOUS SAGITTARIANS: Beethoven, Peggy Woolley, Walt Disney, Frank Sinatra, Brian Aldridge.

★★★★★★★ Ambridge ★★★★★★★

Debbie Aldridge

Capricorn 22 December to 19 January

STAR QUALITIES: Practical, eager to please, reserved, cautious. But Capricorn sometimes pulls out all the stops to make an impression.
LUCKY STONES: Ruby, onyx.
FAVOURITE COLOUR: Dark green.
LOVE: Don't ever let your emotions blind you to the facts.
MONEY: Perhaps it's time to spend some of the cash in your fat piggy bank.
HEALTH: Get plenty of outdoor exercise. Enjoy the sunshine, laugh in the rain and you'll avoid illness.
WORK: Be ambitious, court success, respect authority and you'll get to the top of the ladder.
FAMOUS CAPRICORNS: Joan of Arc, Pat Archer, Helena Rubenstein, Albert Schweitzer.

Roy Tucker

Aquarius 20 January to 19 February

STAR QUALITIES: Everyone loves Aquarians. Strong, forceful, quick and active, but values privacy. Good at partying long after everyone else has given up.
LUCKY STONE: Sapphire.
LUCKY METAL: Uranium.
FAVOURITE FLOWER: Daffodil.
LOVE: You let your heart break silently, and avoid marriage as long as humanly possible. But you never forget your first love.
MONEY: You won't be the best bread-winner around, but may invent something of benefit to the community.
HEALTH: Don't let your absent-mindedness bring on a twisted ankle or broken bones.
WORK: You'll be honoured with some sort of recognition.
FAMOUS AQUARIANS: Lewis Carroll, Charles Dickens, Tony Archer, Vanessa Redgrave.

Tommy Archer

Pisces 20 February to 20 March

STAR QUALITIES: Sympathetic. A quick learner, friendly, kind and practical. Imaginative.
LUCKY STONE: Emerald.
FAVOURITE FLOWER: Waterlily.
LOVE: You see the world through rose coloured spectacles.
MONEY: You are stronger than you think, and wiser than you know.
HEALTH: Emotional or financial worries are a drain on your health. Conserve your energies and don't succumb to other people's pressure.
WORK: Set sensible goals and you'll find recognition and some security.
FAMOUS PISCES: Frederic Chopin, Elizabeth Taylor, Michelangelo.

Robert Snell

Clarrie Grundy

Ruth Archer

Aries 21 March to 20 April

STAR QUALITIES: Impatient, ambitious, full of energy, idealistic and persuasive but exceptionally headstrong.
LUCKY COLOUR: Red.
FAVOURITE FLOWER: Daisy.
LOVE: Scrupulously faithful when really in love; promiscuity or even light flirtation is not on the cards. Love means sharing equally. Unwilling to wait for surprises.
MONEY: Direct in all approaches. Make sure you control the purse strings all the way.
HEALTH: Aim to deter physical disease by positive thinking. You can fight off minor ailments with sheer willpower.
WORK: Bursting with ideas and creative energy, leading others onward to an impossible goal.
FAMOUS ARIES: Harry Houdini, Caroline Pemberton, Tennessee Williams, Phil Archer, Marlon Brando.

Taurus 21 April to 20 May

STAR QUALITIES: Strong, hard working, tower of strength with a violent temper when provoked. Dependable, predictable, equally capable of patching a broken pipe or baking a cherry pie.
LUCKY COLOUR: Blue.
LOVE: A real woman who needs a real man. Your normally placid exterior conceals a sensual nature.
MONEY: A sharp eye for bargains. Try to build steadily for the future.
HEALTH: Miraculously impassive to pain and emotional stress.
WORK: You support your family without complaint.
FAMOUS TAUREANS: William Shakespeare, Elizabeth II, Neil Carter, Barbra Streisand.

Gemini 21 May to 21 June

STAR QUALITIES: By turns happy and pessimistic, outgoing and shy. Gemini – the Twins – changes her mind readily.
RULING PLANET: Mercury.
LUCKY COLOUR: Silver.
LOVE: One Gemini girl equals several women. An expert at the candlelight-and-flowers routine. An active imagination creates many fantasies.
MONEY: Hard to come by.
HEALTH: Bouncing with vitality. Full of life.
WORK: A surprisingly good head for business with considerable powers of persuasion. You'll never be silent when you can speak but find it hard to sit behind a desk for more than an hour.
FAMOUS GEMINIS: Judy Garland, Wallis Simpson, John F. Kennedy, Nigel Pargetter.

Star guide to your character

Jack Woolley

Julia Pargetter

Joe Grundy

Cancer 22 June to 20 July

STAR QUALITIES: A little mad, slightly sad and a bit of a dreamer, drawn to the sea. On the lookout for action and excitement.
LUCKY COLOUR: Gold.
LOVE: Conquer your fears, or your sensitive feelings will be hurt again and again.
MONEY: A capable manager of funds – good at accumulating money and making it grow.
HEALTH: Worry and apprehension may make you ill. Guard against depression.
WORK: You may have inherited wealth and position but you are not content to rest on your laurels. You have to prove you can stack up the gold yourself.
FAMOUS CANCERIANS: Henry VIII, John D. Rockefeller, Ringo Starr.

Leo 21 July to 20 August

STAR QUALITIES: Walks tall and proud with a commanding air and stately being. Stays centre stage with dramatic actions and statements, or by sulking until someone asks what's wrong. Blessed with a strong will.
LUCKY STONE: Topaz.
LUCKY NUMBERS: One and four.
LOVE: Ridiculously popular. Don't blame the lioness for her vanity and arrogance. It's in her nature to feel herself above the common masses.
MONEY: A spectacular gambler at heart, and often wildly extravagant. You're frequently broke, but like all Leos you're sure to line your pockets again soon.
HEALTH: Prone to high temperatures and sudden violent illness. Don't get up too soon. Give time for recovery.
FAMOUS LEOS: Napoleon Bonaparte, Betty Tucker, Princess Margaret, Mae West.

Virgo 21 August to 22 September

STAR QUALITIES: Virgos are analytical in every situation and prefer to keep inner feelings to themselves. Very inventive but sometimes find it hard to make up their minds.
LUCKY STONE: Jade.
LUCKY FLOWER: Hyacinth.
LOVE: You can become the master of the art of subtle seduction.
MONEY: You're not lavish with affection or with spending money. Fear of dependence in old age makes you live so economically as to be called stingy.
HEALTH: Your concern about your own health should prevent serious illness.
WORK: When you say 'no' you really mean it, and you won't go beyond the point of reasonableness. Try not to work late. You don't find it easy to relax.
FAMOUS VIRGOS: Elizabeth I, Greta Garbo, David Archer, D.H. Lawrence.

ARCHERS BOOKS
available from
BBC Worldwide

The Archers: The Ambridge Chronicles

A three-volume novelisation by Joanna Toye telling the story of the Archers of Ambridge, starting in 1951, when the first programme was broadcast, and taking the story right up to the fiftieth anniversary of *The Archers*, BBC Radio 4's favourite drama series.

The Archers 1951-1967 Family Ties

by Joanna Toye

Introducing Dan, Doris, Phil, Christine, Jack and Peggy and their children.

The Archers 1968-1986 Looking for Love

by Joanna Toye

Following the next generation of the Archers as they search for love and happiness in the changing world of the 1970s and 1980s.

Both available now.

The final instalment of the *Archers* trilogy covering the years 1987-2000 will be published in September 2000.

Who's Who in The Archers

by Keri Davies

An A-Z pocket book listing the characters and places that appear in *The Archers* – the perfect guide for both newcomers and fans of long-standing.

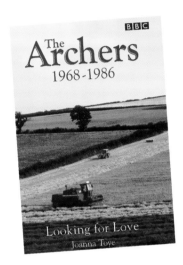

ARCHERS AUDIO CASSETTES
available from the BBC Radio Collection

Abridgements of Joanna Toye's novels are available on audio cassette:

The Archers 1951-1967 Family Ties

read by Miriam Margolyes
4 cassettes

The Archers 1968-1986 Looking for Love

read by Stella Gonet
4 cassettes

Both available now. The third volume will be published in September 2000.

Other audio cassettes available from BBC Radio Collection:

Vintage Archers Volume One

Vintage Archers Volume Two

Vintage Archers Volume Three

Vintage Archers: The Lost Episodes

The Archers: The Third Generation

Lynda Snell's Heritage of Ambridge

The Ambridge Collection

Exclusive gifts from  The Official Archers Fan Club

If you're a follower of *The Archers* you can surround yourself with all sorts of goodies – most available exclusively from Archers Addicts.

When you spring out of bed in the morning, a mugful of tea out of an Archers Addicts mug sets you up for the day. Then it's a quick scan of the *Ambridge Village Voice* or *Borchester Echo*, and on with your dum-di-dum tee shirt and cricket hat if it's summer, Borchester rugby shirt if it's winter.

Perhaps you're on holiday, so check the date on your Archers Radio Times calendar, then take a wander round the countryside with the Plan of Ambridge, Borsetshire County, and Borchester Town Centre at hand to keep you on the proper path.

Carry home your supper in your special Archers tote bag and make sure you're wearing the all-protective pvc-coated apron – as worn by Phil Archer when cooking up treats for Jill.

And now a chance to relax. If you enjoy sewing, The Archers of Ambridge needlepoint kit will keep you busy, but the discriminating collector will be smiling over The Ambridge Bus, The Bull ornamental teapot and the Ambridge horse brass.

Time to put on your Grey Gables bathrobe (in peach, blue or white) and go off to bed with a mug of hot chocolate in a Simon Drew special mug, and hopefully the answer to the question you've been pondering throughout the day. Is the man in your life wearing those gorgeous Archers boxer shorts?

For more information about Archers Addicts contact us:
By phone: 0121 683 1951
By fax: 0121 683 1955
Or write to:
Archers Addicts
PO Box 1951
Moseley
Birmingham B13 9DD

As a member, you will receive four issues of the *Borchester Echo*, Ambridge's fictional newspaper, filled with fun, facts and real Ambridge news. You'll also receive a welcome letter, four quarterly newsletters, *The Ambridge Village Voice*, a membershiip card, a gold-plated enamel lapel badge, and you'll get early notification, priority and special prices for Archers events. You'll also enjoy 10% discount on all merchandise.

Membership costs just £15.50 (UK), £19.00 (EU) and £22 (Rest of the World). Membership is renewable annually.

For up-to-date news of *Archers* activities take a look a the Archers Addicts Website http://www.archers-addicts.com or e-mail us with your views at dum.di.dum@archers-addicts.com

You can get a daily synopsis and news from Ambridge on the BBC's Archers website:
http://www.bbc.co.uk/radio4/archers

This book is published to accompany the BBC Radio 4 serial *The Archers*.
The Editor of *The Archers* is Vanessa Whitburn.

Published by BBC Worldwide Ltd,
Woodlands, 80 Wood Lane,
London W12 0TT

First published 1999
Copyright © Kate Willmott with Hedli Niklaus 1999
The moral right of the authors has been asserted.

All photographs © BBC, except the following:
p.2 © Steve Pyke; p.11 (Joanna Trollope) courtesy Sarah Shearer/Bloomsbury; p.20 © ET Archive; p.52 (T. Meats) courtesy Sue Hammer management; pp 66-8 Archers Addicts/Kate Willmott/Hedli Niklaus; p.76 © Marcus Massey; p.86 courtesy Lorraine Hilton management; pp 94-5 Archers Addicts/Kate Willmott/Hedli Niklaus.

Special photography by Tino Tedaldi pages 4-9, 48-51, 59-63, 73 © BBC 1999
Cartoons pages 3, 19, 27, 45, 72, 78
© Kipper Williams 1999

ISBN 0 563 38415 8

Commissioning Editor: Anna Ottewill
Project Editor: Lara Speicher
Editor: Rupert Smith
Art Director: Lisa Pettibone
Designer: Bobby Birchall, DW Design, London

Printed and bound in France by Imprimerie Pollina s.a.
Colour separations by Imprimerie Pollina s.a.
Cover printed by Imprimerie Pollina s.a.

Cover CD: *Debbie's Diary*
Read by Tamsin Greig (Debbie Aldridge)
Written by Caroline Harrington
Produced by Alec Reid

Acknowledgements
Our thanks to editor Vanessa Whitburn for her kind Foreword, to senior producer Keri Davies for his input and advice on the proofs, agricultural story editor Graham Harvey, *The Archers* production team, scriptwriters and advisers, and to Camilla Fisher, archivist, and Sandie Jefford from the press office, for their help in accessing BBC photographs. To Stephen Fry for his crossword, Stefan Buczacki for improving Ambridge's gardens, Alice Beer, Adam Faith, Alan Titchmarsh, Wendy Richard, Norma Major, Ned Sherrin and Joanna Trollope for joining in the fun, Usha Bahl for her help with the Diwali pages and Agnes Wooldridge for creating the Archers Addicts scarf. Especial thanks to David Willmott for his photographic input and support and to Leon Tanner for his. Our gratitude to loyal addicts Neville Withers, for his photographs of Wood Norton, and Peter Tewkesbury, for allowing us to access his unique collection of Archers memorabilia.

Thanks to Joanna Farrow for the recipe on p.40 and to BBC Good Food Magazine for the photos on pp 40-2; to Roy Barnes for the illustration on p.55; to BBC Gardeners' World Magazine for the photos on pp 71-2.

QUIZ ANSWERS

HOME FARM

Q 1) Naval.
Q 2) Caroline Bone.
Q 3) Bellamy Estate.
Q 4) A solar heated swimming pool.
Q 5) Roger Travers-Macy.
Q 6) Exeter.
Q 7) Grey Gables.
Q 8) They were held hostage in a raid on the village shop.
Q 9) Paddy Redmond.
Q 10) Jack Archer.
Q 11) Eva Lenz.
Q 12) Cheltenham Ladies College.
Q 13) Trout.
Q 14) Alice.
Q 15) He was struck by a cow suffering from mad cow disease.
Q 16) Baby.
Q 17) Deer.
Q 18) Peggy Woolley.
Q 19) Lilian Bellamy.
Q 20) John Tregorran.

BRIDGE FARM

Q 1) Helen.
Q 2) Wales.
Q 3) The ladies' football team.
Q 4) *The Guardian*.
Q 5) A college lecturer Pat almost had an affair with.
Q 6) Jennifer Aldridge and Lilian Bellamy.
Q 7) He was the previous tenant.
Q 8) Organic.
Q 9) His grandmother.
Q 10) Corfu.
Q 11) John.
Q 12) His pork.
Q 13) Sharon Richards.
Q14) Helen.
Q 15) Mrs P's cat.
Q 16) He proposed to Hayley Jordan.
Q 17) April Cottage.
Q 18) Eric the boar.
Q 19) Jam.
Q 20) Blossom Hill Cottage.

BROOKFIELD

Q 1) Lawson-Hope.
Q 2) 1955.
Q 3) His uncle.
Q 4) Phil Archer. (He thought it was Shula!)
Q 5) His hip.
Q 6) Lynda Snell.
Q 7) He joined the Merchant Navy.
Q 8) Birmingham New Street.
Q 9) Elizabeth.
Q 10) A motorway service station.
Q 11) Sophie Barlow.
Q 12) Northumberland.
Q 13) Harper Adams.
Q 14) Rodway and Watson.
Q 15) Jethro Larkin.
Q 16) Christine Barford.
Q 17) She started offering farm holiday accommodation.
Q 18) The last pair of working horses at Brookfield.
Q 19) The Borchester Echo.
Q 20) Glebe Cottage.

GRANGE FARM

Q 1) Dolly Treadgold.
Q 2) Jolene Rogers (The Lily of Layton Cross).
Q 3) Because a female ferret is a *jill*.
Q 4) John Peel.
Q 5) Aladdin.
Q 6) Rosie.
Q 7) To fit into her wedding dress.
Q 8) Jethro Larkin.
Q 9) Susan.
Q 10) Farmer's lung.
Q 11) Caroline Pemberton.
Q 12) A dead pea hen.
Q 13) France.
Q 14) Alf.
Q 15) Great Yarmouth.
Q 16) Eddie Grundy, of course.
Q 17) Britt Ekland.
Q 18) Japan versus Jamaica.
Q 19) The Norfolk lavender fields.
Q 20) Gyp.

CROSSWORD ANSWERS